FEMINIST THEOLOGIES
THE BASICS

For most of Christian history, theology has been written primarily by men. Beginning in the early 1960s, feminists identified ways traditional theologies omitted, ignored, and vilified women's experiences, issues, and perspectives. In the past 60 years, feminists have developed a vibrant theological tradition that is essential for a full understanding of Christian theologies. Feminist theologies engage some of the most important and controversial issues of our time, from the roles of women in society to sexuality, abortion, gender identity, and the environment. *Feminist Theologies: The Basics* aims to:

- Provide historical context for the development of feminist theology
- Examine feminist theological methods
- Share new and emerging feminist voices
- Focus on the feminist concept of intersectionality
- Use the idea of justice to understand feminist theologies.

With definitions of key terms and suggestions for further reading throughout, this book is an ideal starting point for anyone seeking a full introduction to feminist theologies, as well as broader themes in theology, gender, and sexuality.

Susan M. Shaw is Professor Emerita of Women, Gender, and Sexuality Studies at Oregon State University, USA, and is the co-author with Grace Ji-Sun Kim of *Surviving God: A New Vision of God Through the Eyes of Sexual Abuse Survivors* and *Intersectional Theology: An Introductory Guide*.

Grace Ji-Sun Kim is Professor of Theology at Earlham School of Religion. She is the author of over two dozen books, most recently, *Earthbound* and *When God Became White*. Kim is the host of Madang Podcast, which is sponsored by the Christian Century. She blogs on her Substack: *Loving Life* and has appeared on MSNBC, PBS, and C-Span, and writes for *Good Faith Media*.

THE BASICS

BAHA'I FAITH
CHRISTOPHER BUCK

THOMAS AQUINAS
FRANKLIN T. HARKINS

BIBLE AND FILM
MATTHEW S. RINDGE

RELIGION AND FILM
JEANETTE REEDY SOLANO

SECULARISM
JACQUES BERLINERBLAU

NEW RELIGIOUS MOVEMENTS
JOSEPH LAYCOCK

FILM MUSIC
KENNETH LAMPL

JEWISH ETHICS
GEOFFREY D. CLAUSSEN

QUAKERISM (SECOND EDITION)
MARGERY POST ABBOTT AND CARL ABBOTT

SIKHISM
NIKKY-GUNINDER KAUR SINGH AND ELEANOR NESBITT

ORTHODOX CHRISTIANITY
NICHOLAS E. DENYSENKO

FEMINIST THEOLOGIES
SUSAN M. SHAW AND GRACE JI-SUN KIM

For more information about this series, please visit: https://www.routledge.com/The-Basics/book-series/B

FEMINIST THEOLOGIES
THE BASICS

Susan M. Shaw and Grace Ji-Sun Kim

LONDON AND NEW YORK

Designed cover image: Getty Images

First published 2026
by Routledge
4 Park Square, Milton Park, Abingdon, Oxon OX14 4RN

and by Routledge
605 Third Avenue, New York, NY 10158

Routledge is an imprint of the Taylor & Francis Group, an informa business

© 2026 Susan M. Shaw and Grace Ji-Sun Kim

The right of Susan M. Shaw and Grace Ji-Sun Kim to be identified as authors of this work has been asserted in accordance with sections 77 and 78 of the Copyright, Designs and Patents Act 1988.

All rights reserved. No part of this book may be reprinted or reproduced or utilized in any form or by any electronic, mechanical, or other means, now known or hereafter invented, including photocopying and recording, or in any information storage or retrieval system, without permission in writing from the publishers.

For Product Safety Concerns and Information please contact our EU representative GPSR@taylorandfrancis.com. Taylor & Francis Verlag GmbH, Kaufingerstraße 24, 80331 München, Germany.

Trademark notice: Product or corporate names may be trademarks or registered trademarks, and are used only for identification and explanation without intent to infringe.

British Library Cataloguing-in-Publication Data
A catalogue record for this book is available from the British Library

Library of Congress Cataloging-in-Publication Data
Names: Shaw, Susan M. (Susan Maxine), 1960- author |
Kim, Grace Ji-Sun, 1969- author
Title: Feminist theologies : the basics / Susan M. Shaw and Grace Ji-Sun Kim.
Description: Abingdon, Oxon : Routledge, 2026. | Includes bibliographical references and index.
Identifiers: LCCN 2025034923 (print) | LCCN 2025034924 (ebook) |
ISBN 9781032643892 hardback | ISBN 9781032643908 paperback |
ISBN 9781032643939 ebook
Subjects: LCSH: Feminist theology
Classification: LCC BT83.55 .S53 2026 (print) | LCC BT83.55 (ebook)
LC record available at https://lccn.loc.gov/2025034923
LC ebook record available at https://lccn.loc.gov/2025034924

ISBN: 978-1-032-64389-2 (hbk)
ISBN: 978-1-032-64390-8 (pbk)
ISBN: 978-1-032-64393-9 (ebk)

DOI: 10.4324/9781032643939

Typeset in Sabon
by KnowledgeWorks Global Ltd.

Dedicated to Elisabeth Sophia Lee (Grace), and those feminist theologians, past, present, and future who fight the good fight and keep faith in the possibility of a world of inclusion, equity, and justice (Susan).

CONTENTS

	Acknowledgments	x
1	Introduction to Feminist Theologies	1
2	Feminist Perspectives on the Bible	23
3	Asian American Feminist Theology	51
4	Womanist Theologies	73
5	Ecofeminist Theologies	87
6	Postcolonial Feminist Theologies	106
7	Latina Feminist Theologies	123
8	African Women's/Feminist Theologies	137
9	Queer Feminist Theologies	155
10	Feminist Disability Theologies	173
	Epilogue Feminist Theologies: A Path Toward Liberation and Justice	188
	Index	191

ACKNOWLEDGMENTS

We have been writing together as friends and colleagues for over a decade now, and so, when Routledge editor Rebecca Clintworth invited us to write a proposal for *Feminist Theologies: The Basics*, we were thrilled. We are excited to offer an accessible, introductory-level overview of the field of feminist theologies.

We begin by expressing gratitude to all of those feminist theologians whose resistance, creativity, and innovation have created a vibrant field of study that challenges the dominance of white, cisgender, heteropatriarchal theologies that have often contributed to exclusion and injustice for women and LGBTQI+ people across all of their differences. Because feminist theologies are contextual theologies, we need each voice to give us a different angle or a new way of thinking about theology. Theology is an act of imagination. It is an endeavor to name the Divine, to reflect on the sacred, and to envision a world transformed by justice, compassion, and liberation. But for too long, the dominant theological imagination has excluded the voices of women, particularly those from marginalized communities, rendering their experiences, insights, and contributions as inadequate, insufficient, or unacceptable.

We must reimagine theology from the perspective of women who have lived on the underside of history. Their voices—rooted in struggle, resilience, and wisdom—offer profound and necessary insights into who God is and how God moves in the world. It is through their lenses that we see a fuller picture of the Divine: a God who heals, liberates, weeps, births, resists, and accompanies. Feminist theology is not a finished project—it is a living, breathing movement that desires diverse women's voices as they challenge the patriarchal center.

Susan is grateful to the Women, Gender, and Sexuality Studies Program at Oregon State University where she has been able to teach courses on feminist theologies for the past three decades and learn with her students as they have explored the richness of the field. She is also and always grateful to her spouse, Catherine Draper, for her unwavering support. No one could ask for a better cheerleader.

Grace extends her gratitude to her colleagues at Earlham School of Religion and to the feminist scholars and theologians who have journeyed alongside her with wisdom, courage, and solidarity. She is thankful to her three children, Theodore, Elisabeth, and Joshua, who have not only supported her theological explorations but have also served as sounding boards throughout her journey, and to her spouse, Perry Lee, for walking with me every step of the way. It is through the continuous support of family and friends that the difficult work of writing becomes not only possible but deeply meaningful.

INTRODUCTION TO FEMINIST THEOLOGIES

Beginning with Jesus' inner circle, women have always been an integral part of the development of Christian faith and practice. Though not named as such by the gospels but rather indicated by her behaviors and Jesus' behavior toward her, Mary Magdalene was a disciple. Lydia hosted an early form of church in her home. Phoebe was a deacon. Some scholars theorize that a woman may have written the biblical book of Hebrews.

Women show up all over early Christian sources. In fact, women were the majority of Christians in the Roman Empire, and their predominance and active roles in the movement led to great derision by contemporary critics of Christianity. As the new religion institutionalized into the Church, however, women systematically lost power as it was consolidated in the hands of the men who led the Church.

As the Church developed in the first and early second centuries, Christian Apostolic Fathers and Apologists (defenders of the faith) began to articulate beliefs and practices into a coherent systematic theology. Theology is the study of God (and related concepts such as human nature, sin, and redemption). Only men were Apostolic Fathers, and, while women were apologists, their work was generally marginalized and ignored by men in power.

Despite their exclusion from the development of systematic theology, women participated actively in religious communities, wrote about their faith, and shaped Christian thinking across the centuries. Christian mystic women in the Middle Ages such as Hiledgard of Bingen, Julian of Norwich, Catherine of Siena, and Teresa of Avila wrote passionately about their personal, intimate encounters with the Divine. Devoted to lives of prayer, contemplation, and service, these women had a great influence on their followers, women and men alike, including bishops and popes.

Still, men and their concerns were predominant in the Church and the development of its beliefs and practices. Individual women may have had influence now and again or served as leaders and members of religious communities for women, but, on the whole, the Church became a thoroughly patriarchal (male-dominated) institution through intentional decisions and actions.

Women's writings were not valued as much as men's, and often these writings were perceived by men in power as a threat to their power. Much of women's writings were lost or purposefully suppressed. As academic texts became prioritized as standards for Christian belief and practice, women's writings, which usually focused more on the everyday, the mundane, the emotional, and experiential, were marginalized.

These trends continued through the 16th and 17th centuries' Protestant Reformation (a religious and political movement that splintered the Catholic Church and gave rise to a number of Protestant denominations like the Lutherans and Presbyterians). While a few offshoots of Protestantism, such as Quakers and some Baptists, supported women's active engagement, on the whole, Protestant beliefs and practices continued the ongoing suppression of women's involvement in the shaping of systematic theology.

The development of theology was also deeply affected by the modern era, which began with the Renaissance and included the Reformation and Enlightenment and continues into the present. Modernism centers individualism, rationalism, scientific method, and the modern nation-state. The idea of the nation-state emphasizes national identity and sovereignty. This emphasis encouraged European nations to expand their territories by colonizing other lands, subjugating their people, and taking their resources. In concert with the political movement to colonize, many European theologians created justifications for colonial expansion by appealing to Divine will and Manifest Destiny. European missionaries aided in conquest by taking a form of Christianity to other parts of the world that taught the subordination of Indigenous people as a facet of Christian faith. Alongside this, missionaries also carried patriarchal notions of gender to other places in the world.

Individualism focuses on individual rights and freedoms as opposed to group identity and communal responsibility. A great deal of Reformation thinking utilized individualism as an approach to theology, making the individual conscience before God the locus of religious authority. At the same time, modernity's emphasis on rationality, science, and secularism demands that the world be explained through natural laws and reason rather than religious belief. This demand led to a shift in systematic theology that relies heavily on greater skepticism and critical examination of religious claims. While systematic theology continues to be primarily the purview of men, this facet of modernism has also opened the way for challenges to traditional theology from those excluded by it. On the other hand, these critical approaches to belief also contributed to the development of biblical literalism and fundamentalism in the late 19th century as a reaction to the challenges of modern systematic theology to traditional religious authority. Modern biblical criticism approached the Bible as any other historical text to be scrutinized and interpreted in light of current scholarship and discoveries. Modern science contributed to these challenges as it explored evolution and the physical world in ways that contradicted literal readings of the Bible that held the book was historically and scientifically accurate. Fundamentalists argued that the Bible was directly given by God and therefore error-free. They rejected any scientific or theological claims that did not align with their literal reading of the Bible. Their literal reading also meant they supported women's submission to men and women's exclusion from church leadership, including preaching and teaching men. These trends continue in today's versions of Christian fundamentalism.

Despite fundamentalist opposition, the dominant systematic theologies in the West continue to operate out of a modernist framework, and they mostly persist in ignoring, minimizing, and suppressing women's and non-Western experiences and perspectives. They also operate to a great extent out of unexamined assumptions of a gender binary and heterosexual normativity. Traditional theologies assume only two genders—women and men—rooted in biological realities. They also assume heterosexuality as the sexual norm and diverse sexualities as aberrations (if not sins). They also assume whiteness. For most of church history, almost all of the men writing systematic theology were white. They assumed their dominant perspectives—white, male, heterosexual—were the norm and therefore true for all people, and they wrote their theologies as if they were universal in their application. This has had dire consequences for people who are not white, male, or heterosexual because their unique experiences become labeled as deviant, problematic, or unimportant. They are judged through the lens of dominant theologies, and they are often subjugated socially, politically, and economically, as well as religiously.

Modernity's emphasis on the individual and critical reasoning, however, has also provided room for women, People of Color, non-Western people, and LGBTQI+ people to challenge traditional theology as normative. Able to assert their right to speak for themselves, marginalized people have begun to claim space to do theology from their own experiences and perspectives that differ from those of dominant theologies. They have also been aided by the rise of postmodernism in the late 20th century. Postmodernism is a reaction to modernism that expresses skepticism toward notions of universality, grand narratives (explanations that purport to provide a theory of everything), and objective truth. Postmodernism also emphasizes that language is not simply a neutral tool for naming objects but rather a system that shapes how people see the world. As such, it is a political tool that can help create and maintain systems of hierarchy and power or challenge and disrupt them. Postmodernism also stresses the significance of difference and the value of diversity, especially in the processes of dismantling hierarchies and power structures. For theology, postmodernism opens up opportunities for diverse thinkers to contribute to theology from their social locations (the mixture of social characteristics such as gender, race, sexuality, social class, ability, age, and religion that place people within a matrix of power and institutions within their society).

This book is a reflection of the influences of modernism and postmodernism on theology as it pertains to women, gender, and sexuality across differences of race, nation, and ability. We define theology as critical reflection on religious faith, experience, and practice. We approach theology as intersectional feminist theologians. That means we center diverse and multiple perspectives, prioritizing non-dominant social locations, with the goal of spiritual, political, social, and economic liberation for all people. Feminism is the movement to create inclusion, equity, and justice across genders and other forms of social difference. Intersectionality is attention to the ways that the complex interplay of social differences within systems of power affects individuals, groups, and communities. Our perspectives are shaped by our own identities and experiences—as a middle-aged, heterosexual, educated, Korean-American woman and an older, educated, white lesbian. Throughout this book, we offer as many other perspectives as we can to introduce you to the incredible diversity of feminist theologies. The book is decidedly introductory. A thorough examination of feminist theologies would require volumes! We recognize this limitation and hope this book encourages you to explore the wide variety of feminist theological thinking in greater depth by reading the authors to whom we refer as well as the many theologians and feminist theologies space does not allow us to mention.

In each chapter, we will highlight some of the challenges, problems, and critiques that feminist theologians have made against dominant patriarchal Christian theologies and explore some of the alternative ways of thinking about God they offer from their particular social locations and perspectives. One of the important characteristics of these intersectional feminist theologies is that they do not assume a universal "women's experience." While they focus on women, they are careful to recognize that women's experiences are shaped by intersections with race, sexuality, social class, ability, age, and nation of origin. In fact, they often challenge the notion of "woman" itself, arguing that the idea of "woman" as a biological reality is not accurate. Rather, "woman" is a socially constructed concept. This approach recognizes that biology is more complicated than a simple binary male/female, and biology does not have meaning apart from the meaning humans give to it. While we assume "woman" refers to biological features, it, in fact, carries all the meanings attached to the term by its culture. For example, in the dominant US culture, "woman" carries the connotation of feminine. Feminine in this context means soft, gentle, quiet, pretty, demur, sweet, and the like. In some Christian subcultures, "woman" also means subordinate and submissive. Feminists challenge this gender essentialism—the idea that gender is rooted in biology and is fixed and unchangeable. Certainly, the reality of intersex people undermines this idea on a biological level alone. The variety of combinations of biological sex characteristics is astounding when we consider internal and external sex characteristics, hormones, and chromosomes. While biologists debate what constitutes "intersex," estimates are that people born with some variation from strictly biological male or female are about 1.7% or 1.7 people out of 100. Feminists also argue that, beyond biology, gender is much more complicated because culture shapes how people understand and experience their biology and how social relationships between people with these biologies are structured, especially when we consider the intersections of other forms of social difference.

That recognition shapes the structure of this book. Each chapter offers summaries of feminist theologies from these different social locations at the intersection of gender with race, nation, sexuality, ability, and social class because these differences lead people to think differently about theological questions. While we highlight some facets of these theologies (say, race or ability or sexuality), within those theologies, the focus is a matter of emphasis, and the theologies consider intersections of other differences within this emphasis. The reason we use the term "feminist theologies" instead of "feminist theology" is because there is not one single feminist theology, but, rather, there are many feminist theologies that emerge from and speak to the very specific contexts of the people doing theology. While that challenges our comfortable notions of "one right way" of thinking about God, it's also exciting because it means we can all learn from perspectives that are very different from our own that will contribute to a more nuanced and complex perception of God.

These theologies, while quite different from one another, share some overlapping concerns, questions, and methods. Feminist theologians share a recognition that patriarchy is the predominant global system, shaped by other social differences. Feminist theologians are concerned about what constitutes power and how power is distributed and used. They also share concerns about issues that particularly affect women, such as poverty, gender violence, mothering, family, and war. How they think about these things, however, is shaped by their social locations and relations to the topics. Feminist theologians also center liberation for all people in their thinking, though, again, what liberation looks like varies across social locations. Feminist theological methods focus on women—across all of their differences—and begin, not in texts or dogmas but in the lived experiences of women. Feminist methods expand on traditional theologies by valuing what is often excluded in traditional methods, such as personal narrative, Indigenous methods, journaling and memoir, neglected histories, art, and poetry. Feminist theologies root themselves firmly in the everyday, the mundane, and the body, all things often associated with women and spurned by dominant theologies.

Our approach in this book aligns with these concerns. While each chapter addresses these issues of patriarchy, power, and issues for women, the chapters vary in their construction to allow the theologies from these diverse social locations to shape the chapter. As you read, you'll find overlap and difference, complement and contradiction. We hope each of these theologies will challenge you to think more deeply about issues of gender and sexuality and to become more engaged in your own liberatory thinking and action.

Understanding feminist theologies is an important facet of social justice because so often the Christian church has used traditional theologies to subordinate women, LGBTQI+ people, People of Color, and entire groups of people around the world. Because many Christians readily embrace traditional theologies, they do not even know there are options to theologies that subordinate women and consign LGBTQ+ people to sinfulness and abomination. This book offers clear alternative Christian approaches that are humane, ethical, and liberatory, and challenges versions of Christian theology that, in any way, demean, dehumanize, or subordinate anyone.

INTRODUCING FEMINIST THEOLOGIES

Most systematic Christian theology has been written by men with ecclesial power for men with men's experiences at the center, particularly cis-gender, heterosexual, educated, able-bodied, Western, white men. These theologies have often helped maintain the dominance of some men over everyone else as these men have created God in their own images, ignored the perspectives of minoritized people, and built empires rooted in beliefs about their own superiority. Relatedly and similarly, these men have interpreted the Bible from their own perspectives, as if those perspectives are universal, and have used the Bible to justify their dominance over others. Even in their most benevolent form, patriarchal theologies are limited and limiting, telling only a tiny fraction of the stories of humans in all their diversity. These theologies leave out most of us, and that exclusion is harmful to all people and the planet because it gives some people the illusion that it is their God-given right to subjugate people, amass power and wealth, and mistreat those deemed less worthy and the planet itself.

In the First Wave of the Women's Movement in the USA, early feminists recognized the power of Christian theology in maintaining men's dominance over women. Sojourner Truth, a former enslaved woman and abolitionist, found inspiration in her faith to work for social justice. She also articulated an intersectional understanding of gender and race in her work on behalf of the oppressed. At the Ohio Women's Rights Convention in 1851, she challenged prevailing ideas about racial and gender equality. She said:

> I can't read, but I can hear. I have heard the bible and have learned that Eve caused man to sin. Well if woman upset the world, do give her a chance to set it right side up again. The Lady has spoken about Jesus, how he never spurned woman from him, and she was right. When Lazarus died, Mary and Martha came to him with faith and love and besought him to raise their brother. And Jesus wept - and Lazarus came forth. And how came Jesus into the world? Through God who created him and woman who bore him. Man, where is your part? But the women are coming up blessed be God and a few of the men are coming up with them. But man is in a tight place, the poor slave is on him, woman is coming on him, and he is surely between-a hawk and a buzzard.
>
> (Truth 1851)

Elizabeth Cady Stanton, an important force in the struggle for women's suffrage, saw the Bible as a source that contributed to women's oppression. In response, she published *The Woman's Bible* in two volumes in 1895 and 1898. The work by Stanton and other women scholars offered feminist perspectives on passages related to women in order to challenge the ways interpreters used the Bible to subordinate women. Her work was a precursor to the feminist theologies of the Second Wave.

As the Second Wave of the Women's Movement got underway in the early 1960s, feminists noticed this link between patriarchy and theology and the ways these patriarchal theologies harmed women and other minoritized people. Starting with Valerie Saiving's groundbreaking 1960 essay, "The Human Situation: A Feminine View," feminists began to question traditional theological notions and biblical interpretations, shifting the locus from men's experiences to women's. Saiving noted that when traditional theologies interpret the sin of the Fall in the Garden of Eden as pride, they are relying on men's experiences. Women, she observed, do not often struggle with pride. In fact, she pointed out, women are much more likely to engage in self-abnegation and erasure rather than pride (1960, 100–112).

Feminist theologies, unlike traditional theologies, start with women's experiences. While many early feminist theologies by white women overlooked intersections of gender with race, sexuality, ability, and empire, contemporary feminist theologies tend to be more intersectional, recognizing that experiences of gender are always shaped by race, sexuality, ability, class, nation, and other forms of social difference.

Feminist theologies are contextual—they are rooted in the contexts of those doing the theologizing. Feminist theologies are not seeking to create universal understandings of human and Divine experience. Rather, feminist theologies work to illuminate particular facets of human and Divine experiences that are local, specific, and individual and that speak to shared questions about the Divine, human existence, joy, love, and justice.

Feminist theologies are also liberation theologies—they seek to contribute to the movement toward individual, social, economic, political, and global justice. As liberation theologies, feminist theologies understand women, across all their differences, as an oppressed class for whom God shows preference. In other words, God is on the side of the oppressed, and God calls for the liberation of all oppressed people. Redemption is the present task of working alongside God to bring about liberation. Key themes of liberation theologies are God's favoring of the poor and the oppressed; Jesus' identification with the poor; the imperative for Christians to act with and for the poor; biblical mandates for justice; and the necessity of confrontation or conflict to bring about justice. Feminist theologies draw on these themes to think about women and other minoritized people as oppressed classes alongside the poor.

THE TASKS OF FEMINIST THEOLOGIES

Feminist theologies have two predominant tasks. The first is challenging and critiquing traditional theologies that subordinate women and other minoritized people. The second is proposing innovative theological possibilities by re-centering women and other minoritized people as both the doers of theology and the subjects of theology. While feminists tend to share critiques of tradition theologies, they draw on their rich diversity of identities and experiences to create new theologies that are what we call in *Intersectional Theology: An Introductory Guide* "kaleidoscopic." By that, we mean that theologies are not static. Rather, they are ever-shifting, depending on people, place, time, and culture. The goal of feminist theologies is not to determine the "one right answer" to theological questions but rather to draw on the kaleidoscopic possibilities for liberation and justice that come from diverse experiences and perspectives. Let's take a look at the tasks in more detail.

FEMINIST CRITIQUES OF TRADITIONAL THEOLOGIES

The first task of feminist theologies is a critique of the patriarchal, racist, ableist, heterosexist, classist, and colonial foundations and implementations of traditional theologies. Feminist theologies begin in naming and analyzing the problems of traditional theologies as they impinge on women and other minoritized people from the perspectives of the people most affected by oppressive theologies. These critiques identify ways language, theological categories, biblical interpretation, and faith practices are deployed by people in power to maintain dominance and systems of oppression. They remind us that dominant theologies express and universalize only the experiences of a small fraction of the human population in order to maintain that group's supremacy over others.

1. Because traditional theologies are rooted in the experiences of cis-gender, heterosexual, Western white men, feminists note the inadequacies of traditional theologies to speak to and for all people and the limited possibilities for

traditional theologies to contribute to the liberation of all people (especially given their general utilization in creating and maintaining oppressive systems). For example, traditional theologies often posit suffering as inevitable, necessary, and redemptive. These beliefs can lead to an acceptance of women's suffering at the hands of men (through sexual or domestic violence, control, forced pregnancy, conversion therapy, etc.) as God's will when, in reality, this suffering is a result of patriarchal power and interlocking systems such as church, family, policing, and medicine to maintain normative men's dominance over women and other feminized people, such as gay men, trans and non-binary people, men with disabilities, and Men of Color. Other specific beliefs, such as the maleness of God, the responsibility of women for the Fall, women's submission, and the naturalness of hierarchy, reflect men's desire to shore up patriarchy and their power within it.

2. Traditional theologies have set up false hierarchical binaries, with men's experiences as normative. Within this framework, binaries like spirit/body, thinking/feeling, and separation/attachment are gendered so that the characteristics (falsely) associated with men—spirit, thinking, separation—are given preference and dominance over the characteristics (falsely) associated with women. In fact, the binary of men/women itself is both a product and producer of patriarchy and ignores the ways in which biological sex is gendered and in which gender is socially constructed. This binary makes no room for transgender, non-binary, genderqueer, or gender non-conforming people as legitimate and full human beings, and the consequence of this binary is devastating and deadly for people who are not cis-gender, as well as for cis-gender women. Women's place in the binary is also complicated by race. For example, Black women, by definition within white patriarchy, can never attain true womanhood because they cannot be feminine enough. Similarly, women with disabilities also fail within patriarchy to live up to the demands of expected femininity. Theologies that draw a bright red line between men and women ignore the

scientific realities of biology and the sociological realities of social location to argue for a world of traditional white male dominance that views all others as inferior, aberrations, and even dangers to God's design.

3. Feminist theologies recognize that traditionally theology has been an academic and intellectual endeavor that is not accessible to the majority of people in the world. By keeping the doing of theology out of the hands of people, elite men have been able to control the theological discourse and the implementations of patriarchal theologies in the world, often with the help of those harmed by those very same theologies. Theologies done by academics for other academics without regard to other people ensure theological power over others. Feminist theologies challenge the academic power of traditional theologies by engaging theology as a process from the bottom and the edges, a process done by the "least of these," whose viewpoints are privileged in liberation theologies as those with whom God sides.

4. Traditional theologies have relied almost exclusively on male God language. As feminist philosopher Mary Daly once quipped, "If God is male, the male is God." These images of God as a father, king, lord, and master reinforce notions that men are more godlike than women and that the characteristics ascribed to maleness (strength, dominance, rationality, stoicism, and even violence) somehow are a better reflection of the Divine than those ascribed to women (weakness, emotionality, empathy, compassion). The statement on God in the Southern Baptist Convention's Baptist Faith and Message indicates the depth to which traditional theologies cling to the idea of God's maleness: "God as Father reigns with providential care over His universe, His creatures, and the flow of the stream of human history according to the purposes of His grace. He is all powerful, all knowing, all loving, and all wise. God is Father in truth to those who become children of God through faith in Jesus Christ. He is fatherly in His attitude toward all men (Southern Baptist Convention 2000).

5. Traditional theologies have relegated women, LGBTQI+ people, People of Color, the poor, people with disabilities, and people from the Two-Thirds World to a second-class status. Traditional theologies have banned women from ordination, demanded women's submission in the home to a father or a husband, consigned women to a primary role of child-bearing and child-rearing, rejected LGBTQI+ people as members of churches or even legitimate members of society, supported systems of enslavement and segregation, promoted free market capitalism, and enabled colonization and genocide. In today's political climate, we see rightwing pastors and church members using traditional theologies to decry immigrants from South America, support genocide in Gaza, limit reproductive freedoms, and call for a Christian nationalist state in which only certain men will have full and free citizenship.
6. Traditional theologies have ignored the perspectives of multiply marginalized people and have supported Western expansion and colonialism in the name of God. In particular, traditional theologies have ignored the intersections of gender inequality with colonialism and imperial power. Through the creation of discourses of Otherness and inferiority, traditional theologies have applied stereotypes, enacted violence, stripped resources, and enabled trafficking of human beings by offering justifications for mistreatment, discrimination, and systematic oppression of women, minoritized others, and colonized others across the world. Feminist theologians recognize that patriarchal theologies have economic, political, and global impacts that extend far beyond the church and have profound debilitating impacts on oppressed people.

FEMINIST POSSIBILITIES FOR THEOLOGY

The second task for feminist theologies is reimagining theology as a reflection of diverse experiences and a tool for liberation for all people. In the place of theologies of dominance, feminist theologies offer possibilities for love, diversity, inclusion, equity, and justice. Rather than attempting to name Truth with a capital T for all people in all times and all places, feminist theologies rely on the truths of diverse people's experiences to shed light on human and Divine existence. These truths are partial, incomplete, temporary, and absolutely essential in our processes of constructing theologies that move us toward liberation and justice.

1. Feminist theologies demand self-reflection, an awareness of how one's own social location affects, limits, and empowers one's theologizing. Feminist theologies recognize that we do not theologize objectively. Rather, all of our thinking about our experiences is subjective and therefore limited and, at the same time, filled with possibilities for contributing to humanity's understandings of existence. By paying attention to the influence of our own social locations on our theologizing, we are also able to make space to listen authentically and deeply to the voices and experiences of others, particularly those who are different from ourselves.
2. Because women and other minoritized people have been left out of traditional theologies (as well as histories, literature, science, and other realms of knowledge and knowledge-production), feminist theologians must reclaim women's place and history in theologies. For example, feminist scholars have turned to work by women like Julian of Norwich, ignored by traditional theologies as not real theology, to reclaim the place for this work in the theological canon and explore what it can mean for readers today. Other feminist scholars have turned to Indigenous oral traditions or literature by women and other minoritized authors to validate the theologizing that occurs outside traditional theological spaces.
3. Feminist theologies also call for new readings of the biblical text from the perspectives of women and other minoritized people. So-called literal readings of the Bible have been overtly misogynistic, racist, heterosexist, classist, ableist, and imperialist in their use of scripture to

justify the domination of cis-gender, heterosexual, able-bodied, financially secure, Western, white men over everyone else. While historical criticisms have been less overt and dangerous in their biases, they nonetheless have proceeded without attention to social location and the impacts of gender, race, and other forms of social difference on how we read the biblical text. While the tools of historical criticism are helpful, they do not suffice for liberatory readings of the Bible. Feminist biblical criticism offers critique of the text's inherent patriarchy, highlights the "larger truths" of equality in the text, critiques historical uses of the text to subordinate women, and reconstructs the biblical text as a liberatory tool.

4. Feminist theologies also call men to live authentic lives and to escape the stereotypes that limit them as well. Take, for example, the story of the woman Jesus saved from stoning. While this story risks turning Jesus into a knight in shining armor rescuing the damsel in distress, many feminists read the story as one of Jesus actually rejecting male honor and reordering the social system. One scholar contends that the story implies that men should stop proclaiming their own sinlessness in relation to women and admit their own sinful and shameful involvement with patriarchy Like Jesus, they should break with patriarchy and join in Jesus' radical social revolution (Green 2000).

FEMINIST THEOLOGIES OF THE SECOND WAVE

Feminist theologians in the 1970s and 80s identified a number of important interventions needed in theology to address the exclusion and oppression of women in society, home, and church. Central to Second Wave critiques was the issue of language in general and theological language in particular. Feminists underlined the ways language does not merely name male superiority but also produces it by constructing a linguistic picture of the world that legitimates the existing patriarchal order. Take, for example, these linguistic binaries: master/mistress, wizard/witch, governor/governess, knight/

dame. We also see these linguistic constructions of gender in the ways we think about who is likely to chatter, gossip, whine, nag, or bitch and who is likely to be virile and potent. Feminist theologians pointed out how these linguistic tendencies continued in God-language where androcentric words and descriptions reinforced the maleness of God. In response, feminists emphasized feminine images, including those from the Bible itself, such as *Shekinah*, *ruah* (the feminine spirit hovering over the face of the deep in Genesis 1:1), a conceiving mother (Num. 11:11-12), Sophia/Wisdom (Prov. 1:20), a nursing mother (Is. 49:15), a nurturing mother (Is. 66:13, Hos. 11:3-4, Matt. 6:28-30), and a mother hen (Ps. 17:9, Ps. 61:4, Matt. 23:37). Feminist attention to language allowed feminist theologians to challenge meanings and question the adequacy of patriarchal representations of God. Importantly, it also allowed feminist theologians to uncover the interests served by traditional patriarchal God-language and to destabilize traditional God-language by unveiling the problems, ambiguities, and contradictions of the language. For example, Sallie McFague (1987) called for the creation of new metaphors for God that would provide both a shock and a shock of recognition. She suggested mother, sister, companion, friend, gambler, and the Earth as God's Body as alternative metaphors to father, lord, and master, for example. Feminist theologian Elizabeth Johnson (2011) also argued for new language about God, based not on its "truth" but on its socio-political usefulness. Male God imagery, she contended contributes to the unequal relationships between women and men and is therefore religiously inadequate.

Similarly, Second Wave feminist theologians critiqued traditional christologies for their use of Jesus' maleness to reinforce a patriarchal image of God. Instead, they drew from biblical images of *Hokmah* (Wisdom) in the Hebrew Bible and *Sophia* in the Christian Testament. *Hokmah*, which is grammatically feminine in Hebrew, is central in the Bible's wisdom literature. She is a sister, mother, preacher, judge, liberator, and establisher of justice who exercises creative and redemptive power. Feminists also embraced Christ-Sophia as a symbol of inclusiveness and mutuality. They argued that the reinterpretation of biblical images of Christ was essential for contemporary women as a way to disrupt patriarchal christologies that contributed to women's oppression. Feminist theologian Rosemary Reuther (1993) argued that Christ must be the liberator in the social and political as well as religious realms and that to challenge the oppression of women, christologies must recognize that Jesus of Nazareth can serve as a potential model of redemptive humanity, but, at best, this model is limited by its time, place, culture, and gender. Instead, she contended feminist christologies must create other models drawn from women's experiences (114).

In particular, within traditional christologies and theologies of redemption, feminist theologians noted the problems of the cross for women. In these traditional theologies, Eve's sin in the Garden of Eden brought death, and Jesus' sacrifice on the cross brought redemption. Jesus' sacrifice became the model for Christian discipleship, but this call for self-sacrifice and obedience only intensified women's subjugation under patriarchy where they were already expected to sacrifice themselves and obey men. Feminist theologians called for an understanding of the cross in the context of violence against women. Rather than idolizing the cross, feminists reframed it as an instance of unjust suffering with which women could identify.

Earlier feminist theologians also focused on ecclesiology as a site of oppression and resistance. A primary question was: who exactly is the Body of Christ? Are women full and equal members of the Body of Christ or not? Many traditional theologies excluded women from ordination and leadership in the church. Feminist theologians like Letty Russell (1993) called out the myriad ways the institutional church was fully patriarchal and inherently subjugating for women through its theologies and practices. Many of these feminists expressed skepticism about the ability of the institutional church to transform itself.

While these Second Wave feminist theologies were a radical call for equality, they often overlooked the impact of other social differences like race or nation in their theologizing. They tended to rely on universalized notions of womanhood that, in reality, came mainly from the experiences of white women. The theologies developed by Women of Color in the United States and the Global South provided a necessary corrective to assumptions of shared experiences as women and underlined the necessity of intersectional approaches to theology. We'll explore these diverse theologies in greater detail in subsequent chapters.

INTERSECTIONAL THEOLOGIES

In *Intersectional Theology*, we made the case for all theologies to be intersectional in order to capture the richness and diversity of human experience in our work toward liberation. Intersectionality is a term developed and coined by Black feminists to represent the ways in which systems of gender simultaneously shape and are shaped by those of race, sexuality, ability, age, nation, class, and religion. While these intersections are facets of our identities, as a liberatory theory, intersectionality focuses on these larger systems of power in which people are embedded based on their inclusion in these identities. Intersectionality is not only or even primarily about personal identity. It is about structures of power that maintain control and dominance in the hands of the few by mistreating, constraining, discriminating against, and enacting violence in the service of white supremacist, capitalist, ableist, heteropatriarchy. Intersectionality considers the ideologies and institutions that shape individual and collective experiences within matrices of power and domination. It is a praxis that begins in experiences of injustice and resistance, theorizes from those standpoints, and informs future practices of liberation. Intersectionality is always biased toward justice (May 2015). In other words, the aim of intersectionality as a praxis is justice for all people.

Intersectionality demands that we pay attention at all times to all the facets of systems of power, not only the ones affecting us. At moments, some social differences may have greater salience, but they are still simultaneously shaped by the other systems of power. May warns against falling back into "single axis" thinking—speaking, for example, of gender as if it somehow can exist apart from race, sexuality, ability, and age. Instead, our theological thinking should be both/and. Rather than relying on binary thinking, we should welcome different ideas, even those that are competing or conflicting. The question we ask of their usefulness is not whether they are right but whether they move us toward justice.

Intersectional theologies center these intersections. They do not treat social differences as add-ons but recognize the shaping power of each difference on the other within specific contexts. For theology, this means we must recognize how we are products of our social locations, and how those locations with their attendant power and disadvantage affect our theologizing. It also means we must seek out the experiences, perspectives, and theologies of others who are different from ourselves in order to develop more full understandings of human and Divine existence. We privilege the voices of oppressed people, and we evaluate theologies based on their usefulness for moving us toward liberation and justice.

This intersectional awareness is essential for theologies because without its attention to difference, we find ourselves making mistakes with serious consequences for oppressed people. For example, early feminist theologies tended to rely primarily on the experiences and perspectives of privileged white women. Most theologies have paid little attention to issues of imperialism and are far removed from the daily lives of most of the world's oppressed who struggle simply to survive.

Intersectional theological practices keep us tentative in our claims, aware of the limitations of our own minds and experiences, and committed to learning from others as we engage in struggle with them for freedom and justice. Drawing from the work of feminist writers like Vivian May and Patricia Hill Collins, we developed a series of questions in *Intersectional Theology* that theological thinkers should always ask themselves:

- How does my own social location affect how I look at issues?
- How are theological ideas contextualized?

- What is the history of my interpretive community, and how does it influence my interpretation?
- Am I using single-axis thinking?
- How is my thinking both/and?
- How is power at work in the history of these ideas?
- How do these ideas reproduce or challenge inequities?
- What does intersectional thinking do when applied to this problem or question?
- How does this work shift the center?
- How do I think about this issue in ways that are surprising and disruptive?
- What do other people say? Are they fully intersectional?
- How do I hold multiple and competing voices in mind at the same time?
- Am I acting in collusion with dominating powers?
- How does my thinking radically reform theology toward justice?

As we move through the rest of this book, we're going to examine how various feminist theologies from different social locations address issues of power, sexism, misogyny, imperialism, intersectionality, liberation, and justice. Each theology is shaped by the places people are situated within the matrix of power and domination, and the ways in which people are resisting oppression and building coalitions to make social change.

Before we move into examining specific forms of feminist theologies, however, we want to explore how diverse feminists read the Bible. For most Christians, the Bible is a key source for theology, and, traditionally, the Bible has been read to subordinate women and other minoritized people. Feminist biblical critics offer alternative ways of reading the text that challenge patriarchy and support the struggle for liberation from all forms of oppression.

BIBLIOGRAPHY

Green, Elizabeth E. 2000. "Making Her Case and Reading It Too: Feminist Readings of the Woman Taken in Adultery," In *Ciphers in the Sand: Interpretations of the Woman Taken in Adultery (John 7:53–8:11)*, Eds. Lan-y J. Kreither & Deborah W. Rooke. Sheffield Academic Press.

Johnson, Elizabeth A. 2011. *Quest for the Living God: Mapping Frontiers in the Theology of God.* Continuum.

May, Vivian. 2015. *Pursuing Intersectionality, Unsettling Dominant Imaginaries.* Routledge.

McFague, Sallie. 1987. *Models of God: Theology For An Ecological, Nuclear Age.* Fortress.

Reuther, Rosemary Radford. 1993. *Sexism and God Talk: Toward a Feminist Theology.* Beacon.

Russell, Letty. 1993. *Church in the Round: Feminist Interpretation of the Church.* Westminster.

Saiving, Valerie. 1960. "The Human Situation: A Feminine View." *The Journal of Religion*, 40 (2): 100–112.

Southern Baptist Convention. 2000. "Baptist Faith and Message." https://bfm.sbc.net/bfm2000/#ii. Accessed October 22, 2024.

Truth, Sojourner. 1851. "Women's Rights Convention. Sojourner Truth," *Anti-Slavery Bugle* (New-Lisbon, OH), June 21, 4. https://blogs.loc.gov/headlinesandheroes/2021/04/sojourner-truths-most-famous-speech/. Accessed July 2, 2025.

FEMINIST PERSPECTIVES ON THE BIBLE

As the central text in traditional Christian theology, the Bible has played an inestimable detrimental role in the oppression of women and other minoritized people and the maintenance of patriarchy. In the hands of dominant men, the biblical text has been interpreted to subordinate women in the home and silence them in the church, enslave Africans, carry out genocide against Indigenous people, exclude, mistreat, and torment LGBTQI+ people, discriminate and enact violence against people with disabilities, and wage campaigns of war, and environmental degradation and destruction. On the other hand, women and other minoritized people have also found encouragement and radical empowerment toward liberation and justice in the biblical text. Rather than reading the Bible as a text that supports and enables dominance, oppression, and violence, feminist readers interpret the Bible as a call for authentic living, love for all people and the Earth, and justice as a marker of Divine desire.

Feminist biblical critics recognize that the storytellers, authors, and editors of scripture were themselves socially located in times, places, cultures, and languages very different from our own. Rather than understanding the Bible as a text given directly by God, feminist readers see the Bible as a reflection of the faith struggles of particular people within their own contexts. Like contemporary readers, these people had limited experiences and vision; they were products of their cultures; they had their own biases and prejudices; and all of these things come through in the text alongside their wrestling with how to be the people of God. For feminists, that means that we read the text both for the places it reflects and enables bigotry, discrimination, and violence and for the places it calls us to be our best selves, acting out of love, building just structures, and transforming the world toward peace, sustainability, and justice.

Much of the history of Christian biblical interpretation shows how interpreters, mostly Western men, read the Bible to attain, maintain, and expand power. As the Church organized and institutionalized itself, it created hierarchies and soon relegated women to submissive roles, claiming that, because Jesus was a man, a woman could not stand in the stead of God as a priest. The Church also engaged alongside nation-states and authoritarian leaders to build empires, amass wealth, and extend control over people around the world. For a long time, the Church even kept the Bible out of the hands of laypeople, leaving its interpretation to an educated, male, priestly class that often read the text to ensure they themselves would stay in power.

Biblical texts became justification for the torment and execution of (mostly) women as witches. In reality, these were usually single older women, natural healers, and outsiders who threatened male power and the status quo or who owned land somebody else wanted. Biblical texts were used to justify the enslavement of Africans and the systematic rape of enslaved African women, which inevitably came with the institution of slavery. Colonizers used biblical texts to support the doctrine of Manifest Destiny and the Doctrine of Discovery to justify their brutal and genocidal theft of land and resources from Indigenous people in the Americas and, again, the systematic rape of and physical violence toward Indigenous women. Biblical texts rationalized the imperialism of missionary movements that purported to be fulfillments of the commandment to make disciples but were actually (and continue to be) tools of Western colonization of much of the world. Many people continue to use biblical texts to target LGBTQI+ people as inherently sinful, abominations, groomers, and dangers to children and society. White Christian nationalists at this very moment are drawing on biblical texts to justify limits on reproductive choice, forced pregnancy, exclusion of women from public life, early marriage, challenges to contraceptive access and sex education, and even repeal of the 19th Amendment which gave women the right to vote.

PROBLEMS OF BIBLICAL LITERALISM FROM FEMINIST PERSPECTIVES

Many of these interpreters claim to read the Bible literally. The authors of the Bible, however, never would have anticipated that the text would be read this way. Biblical literalism is a descendent of 18th-century enlightenment. The Enlightenment rejected metaphor. Metaphors were not truths, nor facts. They were not the "real world" that could only be accurately described through literal language. For the biblical writers, any literal meaning of the text would have been the least important thing about it. The metaphors were what pointed to larger truths. The Enlightenment brought with it an over-confidence in the ability of science to describe realities, including history, with absolute accuracy. Something was true, or it was not. It happened, or it did not. Biblical literalists approach reading the Bible this way. They are also trapped by a Greco-Roman view of a perfect and unchanging God. This is hardly the God of the Hebrew Bible, but, nonetheless, it is the God embraced by biblical literalists who argue that, since God is perfect and since God gave the biblical text, the biblical text must be perfect. Certainly, the original readers of these documents didn't read them that way, and the church itself didn't either until the Enlightenment when these assumptions became deeply embedded, to the point of invisibility, in some interpreters' minds. Within a strain of evangelicalism, biblical literalism took hold, with tragic consequences.

Central to literalists' beliefs is the idea that the Bible is a completely divine product. Some literalists will argue even that "God moved the hand that moved the pen," leaving no room for error. These biblical inerrantists believe that the Bible is without error, not only in theology, but also in history and science. That means, for example, in our present political moment, biblical literalists read Psalm 139:13 (For it was you who formed my inward parts; you knit me together in my mother's womb) to mean that life begins at conception, and zygotes and fetuses are full persons deserving the same rights as all human beings—and more rights than the person bearing the fetus who can no longer control their own bodily integrity. Literalists also read Paul's admonitions to the Corinthians to exclude women from ordained ministry; Paul's use of a household code in Ephesians means that wives are to submit to their husbands. Some literalists even argue that, based on Levitical law, queer people should be executed. Interestingly enough, literalists are not often consistent in their literalism. They do not believe, for example, that Christians should give all they have to the poor or turn the other cheek or welcome the immigrant. They are literalists when it serves their own interests in maintaining white and patriarchal dominance. Even women readers participate in their own oppression by accepting and promoting these so-called literalist readings. While, purportedly, they are convinced to do so by faith, white women in particular are often able to access social and economic power through their husbands. Submission is the currency for this access. Rather than questioning the literalism that relegates them to second-class status, they embrace it in a trade-off for limited power within the constraints of patriarchy. Likely, all of this is subconscious. They are acting out of a deeply held and largely unexamined belief that they are following the Bible and, hence, God, and yet this perspective makes them complicit in their own oppression and the oppression of others.

PROBLEMS OF HISTORICAL CRITICISM FROM FEMINIST PERSPECTIVES

Biblical literalists, while the most obvious, are not the only people whose reading of the Bible serves to maintain and reproduce patriarchy, white supremacy, and colonialism. While historical criticism, which emerged in the 19th century, opened up essential pathways to interpreting the biblical text by understanding textual problems, authorship, audience, purpose, genre, and editorial and canonical history, the creators of historical criticism were highly educated, elite European men whose perspectives were limited by their unexamined social locations. Historical criticism opened up biblical interpretation in ways that allowed readers to grapple with the Bible as a human, rather than divine, product. It recognized the ways the biblical text was written and edited to reflect certain worldviews, to explore Divine mysteries, and to offer blueprints for moral and ethical behaviors. It also recognized how the text was also limited by the worldviews of its authors and editors. For example, German Christian Testament scholar Rudolph Bultmann, a product of the Enlightenment, argued that the Bible was filled with layers of myth that obscured the kernels of truth at the core of the text. He said readers should "demythologize" the text or strip away those layers of myth. That means, for example, in regard to the resurrection of Jesus, readers must acknowledge that they know scientifically that people do not come back from the dead. Therefore, the resurrection is not a literal event. In fact, we find stories of dying and resurrecting gods throughout world mythology. What is more important for Bultmann is the kernel of truth that Jesus arose in the hearts of the disciples through their new-found understandings of Jesus' life and teachings following his death.

For feminists, historical criticism has been especially helpful in dealing with those problem passages like I Corinthians 14:33-36, I Timothy 2: 8-14, Ephesians 5: 21-6: 9, and Colossians 3: 18-19 that have so often been used to exclude women from church leadership and force women to submit to men. Historical criticism allows readers to understand how these passages were shaped by the time and context of the authors and audiences that makes any attempt at reading them literally and still applicable in the same ways in contemporary society untenable and indefensible.

Despite its usefulness for feminist interpretation, historical criticism is still limited by its own time, place, and worldview. For example, historical criticism tends to ignore issues of gender, both in the text and in the social location of the interpreter. Since, historically, men have been the ones doing historical criticism, interpreters have not paid attention to passages that are what Phyllis Trible calls "texts of terror." These texts throughout the Bible offer stories of women who are beaten, violated, terrorized, and even murdered, and yet this gendered violence often goes unremarked in historical criticism. Feminist readers, instead, highlight these texts and explore their meaning both within their historical context and within the contemporary gendered world. Another example of historical criticism's limitations comes from the Abraham–Sarah–Hagar narrative. Read traditionally through historical criticism, the story of Hagar is read as a threat to God's promise to Abraham to make him the father of the nation of Israel. Feminists point out that the emphases of the story change if we read it as a story of women rather than Abraham. Suddenly, we have a story of women trapped in patriarchy, even as they are located in differently privileged relationships to patriarchal power. Feminists also challenge the typical glossing over of Abraham's rape of Hagar—an enslaved woman who would not have had the ability to consent. Interpreters within historical criticism may respond that consent is a modern concept and should not be imposed on the biblical text. Yet feminist readers may still wonder how Hagar felt about being forced to have sex with Abraham, whether she wanted to or not.

FEMINIST BIBLICAL CRITICISM

Feminist biblical criticism, like feminist theology, begins in the experiences of women and other minoritized people and reads the biblical text through the lenses of the oppressed. Specifically, feminist interpretation uses a historical-critical approach but with an eye to gender. Feminist criticism critiques the text's inherent patriarchy, highlights the larger truths of equity in the text, critiques the ways texts have been used to subordinate women, and reconstructs texts in the service of justice. As South African feminist biblical critic L. Juliana Claassens (2024) points out, feminist interpreters of the Bible use a variety of critical and creative strategies to construct novel approaches to reading the Bible.

RECLAIMING WOMEN

To read the Bible to dismantle patriarchy and other forms of oppression, feminist biblical scholars and theologians use a number of strategies. Some feminist interpreters start with simply reclaiming the priority of women in the Bible. Rather than overlooking and ignoring these women, as has often happened in literal and historical readings, feminists have moved these women to the center of their interpretation. For example, Carol Meyers' 2001 edited volume, *Women in Scripture: A Dictionary of Named and Unnamed Women in the Hebrew Bible, the Apocryphal/Deuterocanonical Books, and the New Testament,* is a compilation of scholarship on more than 800 named and (mostly) unnamed women in the Bible.

ANALYZING GENDER RELATIONS

Another strategy relies on analyzing gender relations in the text. This approach focuses on the dynamics of gender in biblical stories, especially in the ways women are oppressed, marginalized, and victimized within the androcentric frameworks of the Bible. For example, if we pay attention to gender relations in the story of Dinah in Genesis 34, we discover that Dinah eventually disappears from her own story after her rape by Shechem, and the story becomes one of transactions between males. Dinah's brothers take over concerned, not about the harm done to their sister, but about the insult to them from another man diminishing the value of the family's property.

LEARNING FROM WOMEN IN PATRIARCHY

Feminist interpreters also read the Bible to glean what we can learn from women in patriarchy. Women in the Bible are trapped within patriarchy. Yet within those constraints they often act with agency and resistance. Even when they are destroyed by patriarchy and disappear from the text, reading them with a feminist eye lets us learn about living within the confines of patriarchy and learning to resist and dismantle it. To return to the Hagar story, we find Hagar and Sarah trapped within patriarchy. Yet we also find a counter-narrative in this story in which God comes to Hagar to reassure her. Hagar then names God. Still, we find a great deal of ambiguity in this story. God's preferential option for the oppressed seems unclear at best. God meets Hagar in the wilderness but commands her to return to her slavery. God promises safety and prosperity for Ishmael, but Hagar eventually disappears from the narrative, her importance being in her capacity to bear a son. For feminists, reading Hagar's story as a both/and story, one of oppression and resistance, is essential lest readers fall into collusion with the text in our own present situations. The question to ask then of readings of the text is "Whom does this reading serve?" "Who stands to benefit from a particular interpretation and who is likely to be harmed by that reading?"

READING SUSPICIOUSLY

Feminist scholar Elisabeth Schüssler Fiorenza (1983) contends feminists should approach the Bible with what she calls a "hermeneutics of suspicion" and a "hermeneutics of remembrance." A hermeneutics of suspicion begins with the assumption that patriarchy deeply affects biblical texts and their interpretation; that texts must be examined for their possible androcentric bias; and that texts must be examined for both what they say and don't say about women. Silences are important. In other words, we question the narrator; we don't accept his premises at face value. This kind of reading recognizes the patriarchal world in which these stories were told and written down and the ways these stories may have been used then (and now) to subordinate women.

RECLAIMING DANGEROUS MEMORY

A hermeneutics of remembrance reclaims past suffering as a "dangerous memory," one that invites us into solidarity with those who struggle for justice and reclaims the past as subversive, as it also points to hope and liberation. A dangerous memory is a recollection of past suffering or injustice that can empower resistance, disruption, and transformation of existing power structures. The story of the widow and the unjust judge in Luke 18:2-5 is a dangerous memory. In this story, a widow, one of the least powerful members of her society, who has been harmed by an opponent, persists in challenging a judge to grant her justice. While the judge himself admits he does not fear God or respect anyone, he decides to grant the woman justice so she will stop bothering him. This parable is both shocking and dangerous because it clearly shows a woman disrupting structures of her power to achieve justice for herself within a system designed to obstruct justice for women like her. Another dangerous memory is that of the woman who anointed Jesus (Mark 14:3-9). In biblical times, prophets anointed the heads of kings. In Mark's gospel, we find an unnamed woman carrying out this prophetic function. Also, at this time, the anointing of feet was done by social inferiors—slaves or women. In John's gospel (John 12: 1-8), we find Mary, the sister of Martha and Lazarus, anointing not the head but the feet of Jesus. By the time of the writing of this gospel, 20–30 years after Mark's, the church was struggling with the issue of women in leadership. John's account, then, potentially serves to minimize women's role in the Jesus movement. Even Mark's gospel interprets the woman's act as one of preparation for burial—women's work. The dangerous memory of the synoptic gospels, however, offers liberatory possibilities to reading this story. Jesus' own evaluation of the woman's act contrasts with the grumbling of the disciples about wasted resources. Of course, some traditional readers have read Jesus' response that the poor will always be with us as an excuse to refrain from participating in struggles for economic justice and the end of poverty. Feminist liberatory readings, however, offer the possibility that the story actually underlines the requirement for helping the poor as a constant and demonstrates that people can both work to change structural conditions that oppress and, at the same time, engage in personal acts of love for those closest to them.

READING AGAINST THE GRAIN

Reading against the grain is another feminist approach to the Bible. Within patriarchy, we've all been taught to read the biblical text through the eyes and experiences of straight white European men. Reading against the grain means stopping to rethink how we've been taught to read, interpret, and understand the text. Instead of assuming white/cis-gender/able-bodied/wealthy/heterosexual/male perspectives, we choose purposefully to read through diverse eyes and experiences. We pay attention to ways gender is at work in the text and how reading through the lens of gender brings deeper insights, meaning, and depth to the biblical passages and stories.

For example, we've typically been taught to read Eve as a temptress, the cause for the Fall of humankind in the Garden of Eden, a weak woman who was susceptible to the serpent's temptations. If we read Eve against the grain, however, we discover that Genesis contains two creation accounts deriving from different traditions that were combined together by a later editor. Patriarchal interpretations focus on the second creation account in Genesis 2 and its explanation that Eve was created from Adam's rib as his helper. The first creation account in Genesis 1, however, tells a different story. It tells us that females and males were created together in the image of God. Reading against the grain leads us to ask why traditional interpretation favors the second creation account over the first in relation to the creation of the woman. Secondly, a quick look at the phrase *ezer kenegdo*, which is translated as "helper" in English, shows us that elsewhere in the Hebrew Bible, the same phrase is used to describe God. A better translation of helper is an equal partner who supports and protects.

Turning to the story of the Fall, reading against the grain becomes even more telling. This story has long been used to justify women's subordination. Traditional interpretations read the story to say that because of Eve's participation in the Fall, she is condemned to be ruled over by her husband. When we read suspiciously, we discover that in actuality, the text does not say that the woman brings about judgment on all humanity. The text also does not say that Eve in any way seduced Adam to eat the fruit; that Eve even knew of the commandment not to eat of the fruit; that the serpent is evil; that Adam in any way tried to intervene or stop Eve (It does say that he was with her when she spoke with the serpent); or that Eve or Adam is cursed (Only the serpent is cursed). Of course, not only do we have to be suspicious and wary of traditional readings of the text, we also have to be suspicious of the text itself because it was written in patriarchy and has a pervasive androcentric worldview. That is why we distrust the text when it tells us that the Fall is the reason for women's pain in childbearing or that women have a desire for husbands to rule over them. Here is another place where the feminist hermeneutic of justice is key. When we read suspiciously, we ask if a text moves us toward or away from justice. If the answer is away from justice, feminists reject that text as a reflection of patriarchal bias.

INTERSECTIONAL FEMINIST BIBLICAL INTERPRETATION

Like theology, feminist biblical interpretation is done from diverse social locations that profoundly affect how people read the text. On the one hand, it means we have to recognize the limitation of anyone's individual context and interpretation, and, on the other, we have to embrace the unique contributions each person can make from their social location. In other words, no one holds the key to a single biblical interpretation, and everyone can contribute to our interpretive task from their individual perspectives. We then hold in mind, at the same time, enriching, often complex and competing, ideas about the text with justice as the criterion for evaluation of the usefulness of the text for liberation.

This contextual reading of scripture is intersectional. It centers the ways social differences within a matrix of power shape readings of the Bible and offers possibilities to add to our interpretive understandings with the inclusion of perspectives far different, but no less valid, than our own. Following this, we offer a brief overview of some of these intersectional strategies for reading the Bible from different social locations and relations to social power.

WOMANIST INTERPRETATION

Womanist biblical interpretation is rooted in and begins in the experiences of Black women. "Womanism" was coined by author Alice Walker to capture the distinctiveness of Black women's experiences as simultaneously gendered and racialized beings within intersecting systems of racism and sexism. Feminist theorist and writer bell hooks calls this system the white capitalist heteropatriarchy. Womanist biblical interpretation uses an intersectional lens, to analyze the biblical text to highlight the ways gender and race shape one another and shape and are shaped by class, sexuality, ability, age, nation, and religion. Black women's writings, including and especially writings that are not specifically academic, theological writing, provide key data for womanist readings of the Bible. These can be works like Toni Morrison's *The Bluest Eye* or Audre Lorde's collection of essays, *Sister Outsider*, or Maya Angelou's poetry. The point of womanist interpretation is to foster Black women's survival and flourishing. Womanist interpretation also talks back to the text. In other words, interpretation is a two-way street. Womanist interpreters do not simply read the text to learn what it says to them; they also talk back to the text, calling out its exclusions, stereotypes, mistreatments, and misogynoir. Central is an examination of the ways biblical texts have been deployed in support of anti-Blackness and the oppression of Africans and people of African descent, especially the sexual exploitation of Black women. The goal is to enlist the biblical text in "making a way out of no way" for Black women, as womanist biblical critics and theologians, Delores Williams and Monica Coleman, contend.

A womanist interpretation of Mark 8:31-38, for example, focuses on the question of the text's treatment of suffering. The text seems to suggest that suffering is not only inevitable but also positive. Traditionally, interpreters suggest that Jesus' suffering and death on the cross were the will of God, necessary for salvation. This means for followers of Jesus, "taking up the cross" and suffering are requirements for faithful living. Womanists, however, question this interpretation in light of Black women's suffering. This long history of suffering demands a suspicious reading of biblical texts that seem to endorse suffering. Instead, womanists see suffering as a manifestation of moral evil rather than God's will. Suffering is, in fact, an inevitable consequence of Jesus' radical justice-focused and anti-imperial ministry. For womanists, suffering then is a consequence rather than a condition of Christian discipleship (St. Clair 2008).

Womanist biblical scholars have made many important contributions to the academy and to the church. Wil Gafney's *Women's Lectionary for the Whole Church for Years A, B, C, and W* brings a womanist lens to help interpret the church's biblical readings during worship. This is important because often worship is the only engagement with the church and the biblical text for many people. By centering a womanist perspective in the lectionary, Gafney challenges traditional white supremacist and patriarchal readings and makes womanist readings available for everyday believers.

MUJERISTA AND LATINA INTERPRETATION

Mujerista interpretation is a phrase coined by theologian Ada María Isasi-Díaz to describe approaches to reading the Bible from the perspective of Latina women in the United States. It is an approach that begins with the experiences and struggles for survival of Latinas. It is a liberative praxis–reflective action that has as liberation for Latinas as its goal. *Mujerista* interpretation is connected to communities, families, and God's daily presence within them in their struggle for survival. Central to understanding this struggle for survival is a centering of the reality of sin as structural. Structural sin is the ways in which discrimination, mistreatment, violence, and death for Latinas are built into social institutions and ideologies that constrain, harm, traumatize, and often kill Latinas. Addressing sin, then, is not about personal repentance and individual behavior, but rather it is about radical transformation of social systems that perpetuate the dominance and oppression of Latinas. The ways this transformation is carried out for Latinas must be defined by Latinas themselves and their present realities and preferred futures. The Bible is useful in this process only insofar as it contributes to Latina liberation. The starting point for interpretation, then, is not the Bible itself, but rather the present situation for Latinas (Isasi-Díaz 1996)

The story of Shiphrah and Puah in Exodus 1:15-22 highlights the two Hebrew midwives who refused to kill the baby Moses at the Pharaoh's command. In this story, *mujerista* readers find two women living under an imperial power who refuse to be co-opted into acting against their own people. Rather, Shiphrah and Puah define themselves as righteous women who obey God rather than imperial power, and, in so doing, their actions redefine power and critique imperial public policy. This story becomes especially powerful for Latinas when read alongside stories of terror for women in Latin America. Between 1960 and 1996, more than 100,000 Guatemalan women were raped during the brutal internal armed conflict between CIA-backed rightwing generals and leftwing insurgents. Between 100,000 and 200,000 people, mostly Indigenous Mayans, were killed or disappeared as part of a genocidal war. The pharaoh asked Shiprah and Puah to participate in genocide, and yet they refused. For *mujerista* interpreters, this story offers encouragement and hope for present-day Latinas in their own struggles against oppression and for survival.

ASIAN AND ASIAN AMERICAN INTERPRETATION

Asians have immigrated to North America for over 500 years. The first recorded arrival of Asians was on October 18, 1587, when Filipinos landed at Morro Bay, California. With the long history of Asian immigration into North America, there is still a lot of racism toward Asian Americans from the dominant white society. Since Asian Americans are viewed as "perpetual foreigners," it does not matter whether Asians have lived in the United States for 400 years or 40 years; they are viewed as foreigners even if they have American citizenship. This leads to grave consequences on their psyche and personal day-to-day living, as Asian Americans are not fully viewed as "American."

Racism toward Asian Americans increased during certain times in American history. For example, during World War II, we saw the rise of Japanese internment camps, which incarcerated approximately 120,000 Japanese Americans in these harsh environments simply because of their Japanese heritage, even though they were Americans. Most recently, during the COVID-19 pandemic, the number of hate crimes against Asian Americans grew dramatically. These hate crimes included murder, as well as physical and verbal assault. Many of these instances were even caught on camera, though most were not. This wave of violence led to the rise of organizations, such as Stop AAPI Hate, to prevent further crimes against Asian Americans.

In a culture of racism and invisibility of Asian Americans, Asian Americans find it important to fall back on scripture for their hope, strength, and power. Their hermeneutical tool is for the liberation and empowerment of their Asian American community, who continue to live under racism and discrimination. Many Asian Americans approach the Bible metaphorically to help themselves understand their contexts and the need to push toward liberation. They try to do this by linking the world of the biblical text and that of the listeners relationally. This relational link is structured on the interaction between text and context, using a to-and-fro movement rather than a linear order that goes from text to context. This can be achieved by retelling or paraphrasing the biblical text (Kim 2002, 283) so that it provides hope and liberation to Asian Americans. This biblical method of interpretation helps Asian Americans to approach the text with new life and with the expectation of hope. This way of biblical interpretation provides fresh ways of approaching scripture so that they may be comforted and encouraged.

In one specific Asian context, Koreans offer a *minjung* reading of the Bible. *Minjung* is a Korean term for the people.

It refers to all oppressed people. It is not a reference to a particular social group, but rather it is a description of a dimension of social and religious reality. *Han* is another important Korean concept. *Han* is the feeling of suffering that comes from unresolved injustice. Women, in particular, have experienced *han* because of the dehumanizing injustice of patriarchy as it intersects with racism, classism, and other forms of oppression. *Han* is resolved through ritual and storytelling.

Minjung reading of the Bible challenges Western methods of biblical interpretation because it is specifically rooted in Korean social biography or psyche. The task of *minjung* interpretation is to encourage the transformation of oppressive social structures in Korea, as well as the internal spiritual lives of Korean people. *Minjung* theologian Andrew Sung Park explains, "The stories of Minjung expose the absurdity of society, the injustice of the oppressor, and the deeply hidden Han of the Minjung" (Park 1984, 9). Storytelling reveals both the history of suffering and courage against injustice. Biblical interpretation illuminates the suffering of the *minjung* in light of the story of Christ.

AFRICAN INTERPRETATION

African feminist biblical interpretation is rooted in African women's gendered experiences of colonialism and patriarchy. Under colonialism, African women have been doubly oppressed at the intersection of Western sexism and racism and African patriarchy. African feminist biblical interpretations offer a critique of the oppressive elements of African cultures manifested in women's lives, while at the same time highlighting aspects of African cultures that respect and value women. Beginning in their experiences of sexism, racism, and colonial oppression, African feminist interpreters offer a critique of the oppressive elements of the Bible and draw attention to places where the Bible has liberating potential. African feminists also emphasize the concept of *botho/ubuntu*—"I am because we are" and "We are because I am." In African feminist interpretation, liberation is a community/collective commitment and activity. Central to this collective understanding of liberation for African women is family. Family is a key institution in African societies, and oppressed and oppressive families help maintain and reproduce oppressive societies (Masenya 2001, 145–157).

African feminists often use a storytelling exegesis to interpret scripture from the perspectives of African women. This can involve reading the Bible alongside African tales or through methods of African storytelling, retelling a story with different or new characters to address a certain audience, circumstance, or contemporary or historical issue, or having listeners make comments and open up the story for a fresh retelling or participate in retelling. Batswana feminist biblical critic Musa Dube says most readers are "ordinary readers" outside the accepted academic methods of interpreting the Bible. These ordinary readers bring "suppressed knowledges" to the task of reading. Reading the Bible with ordinary African readers subverts dominant Western and patriarchal discourses about the Bible and centers interpretations born of struggles with imperialism and sexism. Dube (2001) offers an example of African storytelling exegesis with an interpretation of Mark 5:24-43 in which the woman at the center of the story becomes Mama Africa, who has been made sick by colonialism and yet struggles for freedom and wholeness.

DALIT FEMINIST INTERPRETATION

Feminist biblical interpretation for Dalit women is complicated by the intersection of caste with gender and poverty in India. Dalits are considered the lowest social group in the Indian caste system. Previously known as "untouchables," Dalits still face incredible systemic discrimination in Indian society, despite legal protections against mistreatment. Among Dalits, women rank lower than men, and so Dalit women have been called the "Dalits among the Dalits" (Melanchthon 2004, 215). Because Christians are a minority in India, Dalit hermeneutics must include women of other faiths and secular women as well. Dalits do not look to develop a biblical hermeneutic or a Christian, Hindu, Muslim, or Buddhist theology of liberation before they actually struggle for liberation. Instead, their hermeneutic is developed in their struggle alongside women of other religions or no religion (219). Because Christian Indian women have been dominated in a society shaped primarily by Hindu, Muslim, and Buddhist scriptures, their struggle includes liberation from the oppression of the patriarchal interpretations of these texts as well as those of the Bible. Likewise, Christian Dalits also call on the liberative strands within other religions to challenge their oppression.

Dalit women begin developing a Dalit feminist theology by reclaiming Dalit tradition and drawing on their own histories and strengths. They also must pay attention to how patriarchal Christian beliefs can be weaponized against them, even by Christian Dalit men. Dalit women must be the point of departure for Dalit feminist theologies as a way to empower Dalit women toward liberation. Because a majority of Dalit women are not literate, hermeneutical methods are primarily storytelling. The telling of stories—both theirs and those from the Bible—help Dalit women articulate their oppression, express their feelings, and create inspiration for struggle toward freedom (Melanchthon 2004).

Dalit feminist biblical critic Surekha Nelavala tells her story as a way to interpret Galatians 3:26-28. She finds hope as a Dalit woman who is considered the lowest in Indian society in what she calls Paul's "groundbreaking solution to gender and racial problems"—"disregarding circumcision as a sign of covenant" and "upholding faith, in Christ, and through baptism." For her, this means that Dalit women can "acquire equal status in the household of God" (2019, 401). Of course, the work to achieve this equality in society remains, but her Dalit feminist interpretation offers encouragement for the struggle.

PALESTINIAN FEMINIST INTERPRETATION

Palestinian feminist biblical interpretation analyzes the biblical text through the lens of Palestinian women's experiences under patriarchal and colonial systems. In particular, Palestinian feminist interpretation recognizes the gendered experiences of Palestinian women under the colonial projects that seek to marginalize, erase, or destroy Palestinian identity and people. It also offers critiques of Western feminisms that ignore the impact of historical and ongoing colonialism and calls for action to further the struggle for Palestinian liberation. For example, Jean Zaru challenges the notion that the Bible gives Israel exclusive claim to the land, especially as Israeli settlers move further into the West Bank and the government confiscates land for exclusive use by Jews. She points to the Bible itself and quotes Leviticus 25:23: "The land shall not be sold in perpetuity, for the land is mine; for you are strangers and sojourners with me (RSV). For Zaru, the Bible instead demands justice be done with the land for all people (2010, 126–127). Niveen Sarras reads the story of Jonah as a call for "minorities and oppressed peoples to change their situation and to challenge their oppressors. Moreover, YHWH's own identity as described in the book can be a powerful source of motivation for Palestinian women today to change their situation under their own patriarchal society and particularly under the Israeli occupation that marks their daily existence" (2015).

JEWISH FEMINIST INTERPRETATION

Jewish feminist biblical interpretation seeks to move Jewish women's experiences from the margins of the biblical text to its center. As Judith Plaskow (1990) explains, traditionally, the Torah is held as "Jewish experience," but she notes that, in reality, it is Jewish men's experience. She points out that when Moses addresses the community upon receiving the covenant from God at Sinai, he speaks to men. In this way, the covenant community is, then, male in self-perception, and the Torah (the first five books of the Bible) reflects this understanding of Israel as a community of men. Instead, she argues, Israel must be redefined by including women in the history of the covenant and in contemporary understandings and practices of Judaism.

Jewish feminist interpretation begins with an acknowledgement of the injustices of the Torah for women. The Torah, for Jewish feminists, is partial and incomplete because it represents only a portion of Jewish encounter with God. A reconstruction of the text is necessary to create a Torah that is whole and represents the entirety of Jewish experience that includes women. To do this, women must be allowed to speak for themselves and name their experiences for themselves. This happens through research that discovers evidence of women's religious lives and leadership throughout Jewish history. Plaskow (1991) also warns about Christian feminists' tendency to take an anti-Jewish stance in their interpretation. For example, Christian feminists may blame Judaism for introducing patriarchy into the world or claim early Christianity was less sexist than first-century Judaism (Heschel 1991).

Shemesh (2011) examines the story of Achsah in Judges 1:10-15. She distinguishes two stories—one of men's conquest of the land and another of Achsah's metaphorical conquest which achieves fields and springs for her new family. In another example of reconstructing women's presence in the biblical text, Diana Lipton (2008) writes Sarah back into the story of the testing of Abraham by God in Genesis 22 in many ways that fit within the Jewish midrashic tradition (midrash is a Jewish method of interpretation that expands on biblical stories). Esther Fuchs (2009, 32) explains feminist midrash as a reaction to the rabbinic tradition of midrash. Jill Hammer (2001, xiv) adds that feminist midrash allows women to find their place within a tradition that has often excluded them.

INDIGENOUS FEMINIST INTERPRETATION

Indigenous feminist theologies address the ongoing colonization and threat to survival experienced by Indigenous women and their resistance to gendered colonizing oppression. Cherokee feminist Laura Donaldson explains that Indigenous acceptance of the Bible itself comes with a high price tag because "too often, biblical reading has produced traumatic disruptions within Native socieites and facilitated what we now call culturecide" (2010, 139). On the other hand, however, she notes, "this depressingly long history of victimization should not obscure the ways in which Native people have actively resisted deracinating processes by reading the Bible on their own terms" (139). As Mayan Nobel Peace Price winner Rigoberta Menchú (1984, 80) explains, Mayan people claim the Bible as their own. By finding themselves in the Bible, Indigenous people avoid colonizers' interpretations and instead create liberating ways of reading that address their own present circumstances of oppression.

Australian Aboriginal feminist Brooke Prentis (2021) reads Genesis 1:1-2 from the perspective of Aboriginal Dreaming stories. Dreaming stories are living tradition of Aboriginal stories that create an Aboriginal framework for understanding the world. They explain how things came to be and show the relationships between Aboriginal people and their ancestors. Prentis points to the story of Bunjil the Eagle from the Wurundjeri people as a Dreaming story that Genesis 1 evokes. Bunjil is the creator. Prentis calls Genesis 1 "the greatest Aboriginal Dreaming story ever told" (25). She writes, "When I think of the birds of the sky, my mind, heart, and spirit, are filled with the knowledge of the Creator, but my ears are filled with the deafening screech of the Sulphur Crested Cockatoos as they circle the skies of Brisbane after the destruction of the forests, their homes, to make way for roads" (25).

Māori biblical critic Beverly Moana Hall-Smith (2009) reads the story of the Samaritan woman in Matthew 15:21-28 alongside the Treaty of Waitangi. The Treaty of Waitangi was signed in 1840 between Māori chiefs and the British Crown. The Māori ceded sovereignty, and the British guaranteed protection of Māori lands and treasures. Not surprisingly, the Māori have still often been unjustly treated, marginalized, and harmed. Hall-Smith compares this situation of the Māori to the marginalization of the Canaanite woman. She notes, however, that the woman's challenge to Jesus can compare with Māori resistance to oppression. She finds hope in the woman's healing that the Māori also experience God's love and healing. The biblical story also underlines for her the necessity of justice and reconciliation.

POSTCOLONIAL INTERPRETATION

Postcolonial biblical criticism begins with colonial entanglements of the text—how has the text justified or reflected the taking of people's lands and resources? Postcolonial feminist interpretation also recognizes that colonization is a gendered process, and disentangling colonial legacies requires intersectional feminist analysis. Postcolonial feminist criticism offers several pointed critiques of traditional biblical interpretation: It is identified primarily with the West; it has supported Christianity's universal and exclusive claims; it has supported expansion and colonialism in the name of God; it has ignored or downplayed the imperial settings of Christian origins; it has ignored the impact of empire on ancient and modern texts; it has ignored the perspectives of multiply marginalized people; it has as ignored ways power is deployed in biblical texts; it has as ignored ways gender inequality maintains structures of colonialism and imperial power; it has as ignored or reinforced antisemitic biases in Christian thought; it has created discourses of Otherness and inferiority applied to entire peoples and continents; it has failed to critique the imperialism of the missionary movement; and it has been done through a cis, white, heteropatriarchal lens.

Throughout the Bible, we find stories in which women are abused, violated, raped, and murdered. These stories often happen in the context of an empire, and women are part of what is conquered in the conquest. Postcolonial feminist viewpoints are concerned with the ways power, gender, and colonial concerns are deployed in the text. In addition to critiquing colonial domination in the text, they also offer counter-readings from the perspectives of women in the "contact zone," the places of colonial encounter where people from different geographic areas come into contact with one another, most often in situations of inequality and conflict. Postcolonial feminist readers also scrutinize interpretations offered by other critics for their colonial entanglements, and they emphasize the contributions of ordinary readers who offer unique perspectives from their locations as marginalized women.

If we turn a postcolonial feminist lens on the story of Rahab in Joshua 2 and 6:22-25, we see a clear story of the expansion of empire as the ancient Israelites seek to conquer Jericho. Rahab, as the story tells us, is a prostitute living on the edges of the city. We might ask what circumstances led her into this situation. Perhaps she sees the Israelites as a way out of the mistreatment at the hands of her own people. We might also ask why the Israelite spies were in the house of a prostitute staying the night. Postcolonial feminist readers may evaluate her actions as selling out her own people. Musa Dube notes that in many narratives, women often represent land, and conquering women symbolize conquering land. Rahab's story then both colonizes her as an individual and becomes justification for the colonization of Jericho. Rahab herself internalizes the values of the colonizers, accepting the inevitability of their conquest. Dube adds that a postcolonial reading of this story also requires the creation of counternarratives, stories of the "Rahabs" who have resisted and risen up against colonizers.

QUEER INTERPRETATION

While queer was long a pejorative term for LGBTQI+ people, many within the community have reclaimed the word as a symbol of pride and resistance to heteronormativity, the assumption of and practices and institutions that reinforce heterosexuality. Queer is an overtly political term employed by the community in opposition to heterosexism, homophobia, and transphobia. It disrupts binaries and fixed identities and challenges essentialist notions of gender and sexuality. Succinctly defined, queer is what is at odds with what is "normal."

Queer biblical interpretation interrupts and deconstructs heteronormative interpretations by challenging unspoken assumptions about gender and sexuality in the text and its interpretations, by using lenses of queer experience to interpret the Bible, and by opening up spaces within the text and its interpretations for diverse and transitional sexualities and gender identities, along with their intersections with other forms of social difference. "Coming out" is a dominant metaphor in queer interpretations. For example, queer interpretation can read the resurrection as a coming-out story. Jesus comes out of the tomb, and his resurrection is God's affirmation of Jesus' choice to challenge established norms of imperialism, patriarchy, established religious power, and injustice. Queer interpretation also works to de-familiarize the accepted norms of traditional biblical interpretation. For instance, queer interpretation asks us to imagine Naomi, Ruth, and Boaz as a queer family rather than a normative heterosexual family. To queer the biblical text, readers look for ambiguities in the text, people and situations that can be read as queer, people at the margins of respectability, destabilized categories, and relationships and close attachments. Queer interpretations prioritize texts that contest dominant identities, critique power relationships, and interrupt heteronormativity.

Returning to the story of Ruth, we find a coming-out story on the road from Moab to Bethlehem (West 2006). While Orpah chooses to leave Naomi to return to her people, Ruth "comes out," declaring her true feelings for Naomi, employing the same work, *davka* (cling) used in Genesis 2:24 ("Therefore a man leaves his father and his mother and clings to his wife"). When they arrive in Bethlehem, Ruth goes to a field to glean. When Boaz asks the typical patriarchal question, "To whom does this woman belong?" the foreman gives a surprising answer: "She is the Moabite who came back with Naomi." Boaz responds by ensuring Ruth and Naomi can continue to live together by inviting her to return to his fields and instructing his workers to leave grain for her to glean. Naomi recognizes, however, that she and Ruth need a longer-term strategy, and so she works with existing kinship laws to find a way for her, Ruth, and Boaz to form their own family. Eventually, Ruth and Boaz have a son. The townswomen have an interesting response. They name the baby and say, "A son has been born to Naomi."

ECO-FEMINIST INTERPRETATION

Climate change is one of the most pressing social issues of our time, with grave consequences. It is a public health crisis, and there is an urgent need for us to act so that we can diminish climate change. Some biblical interpretations by white men have propelled us toward this climate disaster that we are presently facing globally. The damaging effects of climate change have greater impact on women than men, and on poorer nations more than rich ones. The need for eco-feminist biblical interpretation is dire to help stop this global crisis from turning into a global disaster.

Ecofeminist biblical scholars and theologians are rereading scripture in light of the climate crisis and offering new ways of reading, which push us toward saving the Earth. We have often misread the Genesis story of the creation of the world and of humanity as a call to exercise domination over the Earth. Traditionally, we have read, "God blessed them, and God said to them, 'Be fruitful and multiply and fill the Earth and subdue it and have dominion over the fish of the sea and over the birds of the air and over every living thing that moves upon the Earth'" (Genesis 1:28) as a command to dominate the Earth. Just as many readers have misinterpreted Genesis to institutionalize men's dominance over women, many have also misinterpreted this passage as a mandate for humans to dominate the Earth. The passage has been misread as a commandment from God to do as we wish to the Earth. This type of biblical interpretation has contributed to this present climate crisis. Eco-feminist scholars remind us that we are not to dominate creation but to be caretakers of the Earth. We are to care for the Earth that God has created, and this interpretation becomes a helpful way to move toward climate justice.

Christian Testament scholar Barbara Rossing offers insight into eschatology as found in the Bible. Rossing reminds us that the eschatology of Revelation is both ecologically rich and challenging and not dreary and destructive as some traditional interpretations have emphasized. Rossing points out that waters and other natural elements speak, represented by angels or messengers, participate in judgment and salvation. The Earth herself, imagined as a female figure, comes to the rescue of the woman (Rev 12:16). There are scenes of ecological destruction and cosmic catastrophe, but that violence against creation represents not God's violence but Rome's violence. It is the consequence of the empire's rapacious system spinning out of control. The New Jerusalem vision of Revelation 21–22 brings heaven down to Earth, making all things "new" in the most expansive eschatological vision of the entire Christian Testament. The healing leaves of the Tree of Life usher us to reimagine eschatology as healing (Rossing 2017, 332) and not as a destruction of the Earth and God's creation.

Reading scripture from an eco-feminist hermeneutic provides life-giving messages in contrast with traditional interpretations of eschatology, which focus on the doom and destruction of the Earth. Eco-feminist theologians point out that eschatology that fixates on the last judgment and the afterlife is especially problematic in the face of the planetary crisis. The visual picture of individuals being judged for their sins cannot account for structural sin that causes so much damage to people and the Earth. It does not address the cruel structural injustice of climate change: that judgment falls not on those who sinned or caused the problem but on the poorest and most vulnerable people of our world. Moreover, when salvation is imagined as the soul going to heaven after death, this can lead to the escapist eschatological thinking of "this world is not my home" (Rossing 2017, 335) and, therefore, I don't have to take care of it. This removes any burden of the consequences of our actions here on Earth, or any responsibility for the Earth's care. If we just focus on "heaven," we will lose our calling to take care of the Earth.

For the Bible to be useful in human liberation, we need all of these intersectional readings to learn from one another's experiences and to become allies across our differences. Because the Bible is the key text of Christianity and because it has so often been used to perpetuate the oppression of women, racism, homophobia and transphobia, and other forms of systemic mistreatment and harm, feminists recognize the necessity of challenging traditional readings and offering instead new feminist readings that are liberatory and life-affirming.

BIBLIOGRAPHY

Claassens, L. Juliana. 2024. "Feminist Biblical Interpretation," In *St Andrews Encyclopaedia of Theology*. Eds. Brendan N. Wolfe et al. https://www.saet.ac.uk/Christianity/FeministBiblicalInterpretation

Donaldson, Laura E. 2010. "The Sign of Orpah: Reading Ruth Through Native Eyes," p. 138–151. In *Hope Abundant: Third World and Indigenous Women's Theology*, Ed. Kwok Pui-Lan. Orbis.

Dube, Musa. 2001. "Fifty Years of Bleeding: A Storytelling Feminist Reading of Mark 5:24-43," p. 50–60. In *Other Ways of Reading: African Women and the Bible*. Society of Biblical Literature.

Fuchs, E. 2009. "Jewish Feminist Approaches to the Bible," p. 25–40. In *Women and Judaism: New Insights and Scholarship*, Ed. F.E. Greenspahn. New York University Press.

Kim, Eunjoo Mary. 2002. "Hermeneutics and Asian American Preaching," In *The Bible in Asian America*. Eds. Tatsiong Benny Liew & Gale A. Yee. The Society of Biblical Literature.

Hall-Smith, Beverly Moana. 2009. "Matthew 15:21-28: Through the Lens of the Treaty of Waitangi." *Mai i Rangiātea*, 4: 31–35.

Hammer, J. 2001. *Sisters at Sinai: New Tales of Biblical Women*. Jewish Publication Society.

Heschel, Susannah. 1991. "Feminism and Jewish-Christian Dialogue," p. 227–246. In *Introduction to Jewish-Christian Relations*, Eds. Michael Shermis & Arthur E Zonnoni. Paulist Press.

Isasi-Díaz, Ada María. 1996. *Mujerista Theology*. Orbis.

Lipton, Diana. 2008. *Longing for Egypt and Other Unexpected Biblical Tales*. Sheffield Phoenix Press.

Melanchthon, Monica. 2004. "Indian Dalit Women and the Bible: Hermeneutical and Methodological Reflections," p. 212–224. In *Gender, Religion and Diversity: Cross-Cultural Perspectives*, Eds. Ursula King & Tina Beattie. Continuum.

Masenya, Madipoane. 2001. "A Bosadi (Womanhood) Reading of Proverbs 31: 10-31," p. 145–157. In *Other Ways of Reading: African Women and the Bible*, Ed. Musa Dube. Society of Biblical Literature.

Meyers, Carol, Ed. 2001. *Women in Scripture: A Dictionary of Named and Unnamed Women in the Hebrew Bible, the Apocryphal/Deuterocanonical Books, and the New Testament*. Wm. B. Eerdmans.

Nelavala, Surekha. 2019. "My Story" in Intersection with Gal. 3:26-28: An Indian-*Dalit* Feminist Interpretation," p. 395–406. In *T&T Clark Handbook of Asian American Biblical Hermeneutics*. Eds. Uriah Y. Kim & Seung Ai Yang. T & T Clark.

Park, A. Sung. 1984. "Minjung Theology: A Korean Contextual Theology." *Indian Journal of Theology*, 33 (4): 1–11.

Plaskow, Judith. 1990. *Standing Again at Sinai: Judaism from a Feminist Perspective*. Harper & Row.

Plaskow, Judith. 1991. "Feminist Anti-Judaism and the Christian God." *Journal of Feminist Studies in Religion*, 7: 99–108.

Prentis, Brooke. 2021. "What Can the Birds of the *Land* Tell Us?" p. 19–30. In *Grounded in the Body, in Time and Place, in Scripture: Papers by Australian Women Scholars in the Evangelical Tradition*, Eds. Jill Firth & Denise Cooper-Clarke. Wipf and Stock Publishers.

Rossing, Barbara. 2017. "Reimagining Eschatology: Toward Healing and Hope for a World at the Eschatos," p. 325–348. In *Planetary Solidarity*, Eds. Grace Ji-Sun Kim & Hilda Koster. Fortress Press.

Sarras, Niveen. 2015. "A Palestinian Feminist Reading of the Book of Jonah." *Journal of Lutheran Ethics*, 15 (8). https://learn.elca.org/jle/a-palestinian-feminist-reading-of-the-book-of-jonah.

Schüssler Fiorenza, Elisabeth. 1983. *In Memory of Her: A Feminist Theological Reconstruction of Christian Origins*. Crossroad Publishing Company.

Shemesh, Yael. 2011 "Achsah, from Object to Subject: A Story About a Wise Woman, a Field and Water (Judges 1:10-15)." *Studies in Bible and Exegesis*, 10: 23–48.

St. Clair, Raquel Annette. 2008. *Call and Consequences: A Womanist Reading of Mark*. Fortress.

West, Mona. 2006. "Ruth," p. 190–194. In *The Queer Bible Commentary*, Eds. Deryn Guest, Robert E. Goss, Mona West & Thomas Bohache. SCM Press.

Zaru, Jean. 2010. "Biblical Teachings and the Hard Realities of Life," p. 123–137. In *Hope Abundant: Third World and Indigenous Women's Theology*, Ed. Kwok Pui-Lan. Orbis Books.

ASIAN AMERICAN FEMINIST THEOLOGY

Asian American feminist theology emerged from Asian American women's desire to carve a space for themselves within this important feminist theology scholarship and discourse. Asian American women experience sexism within their own culture as well as the wider dominant culture. Additionally, they experience racism from the dominant white society, which hurts their personal, social, and religious experience. This chapter will examine the history of Asian immigration to the United States and some of the difficulties and oppressions that Asian American women face. In response to these conditions, Asian American feminist theologians have developed theologies to center intersecting experiences of racism and sexism and to move society toward liberation for Asian American women. These theologies take into account the particularities of Asian American women's experiences and challenge the church to make Asian American women visible in all aspects of the church and society.

ASIAN AMERICAN HISTORY OF IMMIGRATION

Asian Americans have a long history in the United States. While people of Asian descent have been in the United States since 1587 (e.g., Filipinos in California, Louisiana, and Alaska), Asians continued to immigrate to the United States and large numbers arrived in the nineteenth and twentieth centuries to work in the plantations of Hawai'i, the fisheries of Alaska and Louisiana, the railroads, gold mines, farms, and gardens of the continental West, and industrialized agribusiness sites of the Midwest (Ho 2019, 17). During the height of the United States' westward expansion and the building of its economy in the 19th century and beyond, Asian labor became a commodity to be used and traded. The annexation of California in 1848 opened the floodgates for Asian labor and prompted the arrival of many Asians, including Japanese (1880s), Filipinos (1900), Koreans (1903), and Indians (1907), in the United States (Fernandez 2003, 256). Missionaries encouraged Koreans to go to Hawaii, as it was considered a Christian land. An estimated 40% of the 7,000 emigrants who left Korea between December 1902 and May 1905 were Christian converts (Chan 1991, 15). When they arrived, they did not live easy lives as they worked under harsh conditions for little pay. Many of them worked as indentured workers, which is similar to enslavement but with an expiration date. The expiration date depends on whether the workers can repay those who indentured them. Asian American women suffered more as they had to endure difficulties not only from racism but also from sexism.

In the 19th century, Asian immigrants were mostly young male exploited workers. Laws prevented Asian women (1875 Page Law) from entering the country. The 1875 Page Law was originally constructed to keep out cheap labor and prostitutes, but it ended up regulating the entry of Chinese women into the United States. White America feared that the presence of Asian women would lead to the birth of a second generation of Asians in the United States. That fear was unfounded and would have been hard to realize since the gender ratio of Chinese men to women was an appalling 1,685 to 1 in 1852, and 27 to 1 by 1890 (Takaki 1989, 121).

These racist immigration policies had consequences on Asian and white women's relationships with Asian men. In addition to the prohibition of interracial marriage of Asian men with white women, the 1922 Cable Act declared that any woman who married an "alien ineligible for citizenship" shall cease to be a citizen of the United States. This harsh law was meant to intimidate white people from marrying non-white people. The Immigration Act of 1924 forbade women from China, Japan, Korea, and India from entering the United States, even as wives of US citizens. This law was not changed until 1945 with the passage of the War Brides Act, which allowed the immigration of Asian spouses and children of US servicemen. Asians living in the United States were not allowed to become naturalized citizens until the McCarren–Walter Act of 1952 hundreds of years after the first Asians came to what is now the United States. These laws reveal that race and gender have been dominant factors in the formation of state policies concerning the treatment of Asian Americans and, indeed, for the formation of Asian American communities.

ASIAN WOMEN'S HARDSHIPS

Korean women's immigration to the United States was driven by women's desire for greater freedom from the confines of their Asian culture and the constraints of Confucianism on women. Within Confucianism, women are taught to be obedient from a very young age. Little girls are told to be obedient to their fathers, and, when they marry, they are told to be obedient to their husbands. When they become widowed, they are to be obedient to their sons. Within this Confucian model, women are to always be obedient to men, especially the three men in their familial relationships.

The need for obedience by Asian women has fostered their subjugation and subordination. They are required to be subordinate to their fathers or their husbands. There is a strict hierarchy, and women are always relegated to second-class status, which diminishes their identity and self-being. There is a lot of sexist oppression within Asian societies and cultures, which value boys over girls and often value raising geese over raising girls. Women fleeing Asian patriarchal cultures to North America did not find the freedom from patriarchy they had expected, as immigrating to North America did not mean that patriarchal culture disappeared. The United States was a difficult place for women to escape oppression. Even as women fled their oppression in Asia, they found themselves victimized in the United States by men intent on profit and exploitation, which led to tremendous levels of hardships and difficulties (Okihiro 1994, 77).

For example, many Korean women were misinformed as they left Korea to escape patriarchy and to seek freedom from family obligations. After immigration, they found themselves captives under harsh and difficult working situations in the United States. Some were working long hours in the sugar plantations in Hawai'i under harsh conditions. Other women who went to the continental United States were pushed into sex work or worked as indentured servants which involved long working days without pay or with minimal pay. Their new life was unexpected, and many found the amount and nature of the work demanded of them to be unbearable. They also found it difficult to return to Korea, and so they were forced to create new lives as immigrants in the United States.

Asians were feared due to racism, and some white people thought they would bring diseases. Congress in 1882 passed the Chinese Exclusion Act, which prevented any more Asians from coming into the United States. Those who were already in the United States were treated harshly and didn't have the right to vote, buy property, or have the right to fight in court against white people. However, Asian women were allowed to immigrate to Hawai'i in part because Hawai'i was an American economic colony, consisting of only a small percentage of white people, who were mostly men. The fear of miscegenation and the tainting of the "purity" of the white race were not major concerns. Many Korean men came alone and lived in large boarding homes. Since they were single, they needed women to be in the boarding homes to take care of the men. The women who came to take these jobs, however, were misinformed about the expectations of the positions. They were ill-prepared for the hardships of camp, the daily work, and plantation life. Furthermore, the number of women working in the plantations was so low that the burden of "women's work" was overwhelming, tiresome, and oppressive for the few women who were there.

At both camps and plantations, Korean women worked long hours. On the plantation, women engaged in many of the same assignments, such as hoeing, stripping leaves, and harvesting, as men, but they were paid less than their male counterparts. At the camps, women cooked, washed, and cleaned, not only for their own families but often, for a small fee, for the bachelors and married men who had come to Hawai'i without their wives. Those who cooked for the unattached or unmarried men had to get up at 3 or 4 a.m. to make breakfast for as many as 40 persons and to pack an equal number of lunch boxes in primitive kitchens with no modern conveniences (Grace Ji-Sun Kim, 2002, The Grace of Sophia, (Cleveland: Pilgrim Press), 66.) Others who worked in the fields for wages spent a full day under the sun, with babies strapped to their backs, before returning home to fix dinner for their husbands or other male workers. In the evenings, they washed, ironed, and mended. Those who bore children did all this work even while pregnant (Lee 1990). This was a harsh reality that many women did not expect to find in the United States. They left their homeland in high hopes of achieving liberation and freedom from the confines of Confucianism, only to find backbreaking difficulties, hardships, and pain. Furthermore, they also experienced racism from the wider society, which was dehumanizing and harmful to them.

RACIALIZATION AND RACISM

Racialization is a process by which skin color and cultural practices are given social importance as markers of difference (Anderson 1999, 18). Racialized identities are in part the result of how the dominant group has stereotyped minority groups. In the United States, the categorization and racialization of people is done by white people who hold power in society. The Supreme Court in the early 1900s categorized Asians in the United States as not white despite pale skin, patriotic military service, decades of residency, English fluency, American education, and Christianity. Despite individual and collective endeavors to perform what Kimberly McKee calls "cultural whiteness," Asian Americans and particularly Asian American women were juridically disenfranchised as racially Other and segregated as not-quite-white throughout US history and popular culture. Laws and hegemonic discourses of the United States have kept Asian immigrants on the periphery. Many Asian Americans believe that their history is made "invisible" (Ho 2019, 17–18), and women's stories, in particular, have been lost. Many women's stories have been silenced not only in the white society but also within their ethnic communities. This is a way for white people to control the American narrative and American history by eliminating and erasing Asian Americans' place and role in history.

In the United States, racism is a binary discourse. Thus, racism is talked about in black and white terms, and Asian American women do not fall into that space. As a result, Asian American women's experiences of racism are often ignored and diminished. Usually, they are told that their experiences of racism are "not racism" as they are not Black people. They are often told that they are "honorary whites" as if there is a hierarchy of people, and whites are always at the top of the hierarchy. This results in the subjugation and subordination of Asian American women, who are often placed near the bottom of the hierarchy of both race and gender, where they are expected to be silent and obedient. Asian American women must address these intersecting oppressions so that they can work toward some form of liberation, wholeness, and flourishing.

Racism manifests the deeply entrenched determination to maintain the status quo. It has become institutionalized and internalized by those who believe there is a center in society, that they are part of that center, and that they are right to relegate those unlike them to the margins. Racism promotes the exclusion of the vulnerable and powerless from basic social equality and opportunity by groups who believe they are the only ones fully entitled to the benefits of our economic, social, cultural, and intellectual spheres. Racism is an attitude that promotes domination of the vulnerable by a privileged group who regard their beliefs, values, and cultural practices as the norm, according to which other cultures and social practices are judged, objectified, and relegated to the margins (Matsuoka 1998, 3, 143). Racism favors the dominant group and keeps the subordinate group in their less entitled status. Race is a constructed concept that serves those who feel that their positions of power, real or imagined, are not threatened.

OPPRESSIONS AGAINST ASIAN AMERICAN WOMEN

For Asian American women, anti-Asian racism intersects with sexism to shape oppression. Asian American historiography reveals a context that gave birth to narratives such as the racial categorization of Asian Americans as "perpetual foreigners," "non-assimilable," "model minority," "honorary whites," and Asian American males as emasculated and Asian American women as hypersexualized. We recognize that Asian American men were portrayed as feminine with long pigtails and given feminized roles such as washers and cleaners. On the other hand, Asian American women were viewed as prostitutes who existed for the gratification of men. Even though a married Asian male indentured worker desired to bring his wife with him, US immigration laws made it nearly impossible for him to do so. Hence, US immigration laws and acts shaped the gender composition and social class of Asian American communities in the United States.

During the COVID-19 pandemic, Asian American women were randomly targeted and assaulted as a result of the widely shared falsehood that China was to blame for the pandemic. These unprovoked physical and verbal assaults occurred in public and were caught on camera and cell phones. Asian American women were molested while walking on the sidewalk or riding on subways and buses. Unfortunately, many assaults were not caught on camera, and some Asian American women were murdered. The rise of AAPI hate crimes increased rapidly, and many of them were committed against Asian American women.

ASIAN AMERICAN EXPERIENCES OF RACISM

In many ways, Asian Americans' experiences of racism vary from those of other people of color because of the ways Asians are categorized and stereotyped differently based on race.

Asian Americans are often labeled "honorary whites," which reinforces a hierarchy of people with the white people at the top of the hierarchy. Asian Americans are not white, but they are "almost" white, which places them higher in the racial hierarchy than black people. By labeling Asian Americans as honorary whites, the dominant culture positions them as less than white people but better than black people. This tactic also serves to "divide and conquer" by pitting diverse people of color against one another.

During the 1960s, white sociologists came up with the term "model minority" to define, describe, and label Asian Americans. It was a term of division and divisiveness as it was used to compare Asian Americans to other people of color. When those in power get to define others, they are able to maintain their power. The model minority myth was to tell other people of color, "If you work as hard as Asian Americans, you will be rich. If you study as hard as Asian Americans, you will get into the top schools. If you try as hard as Asian Americans, you will succeed." This is a false narrative ignored differences across Asian Americans, overlooked Asian American struggles, and blamed other people of color for their own difficulties. By pitting people of color against one another, dominant culture creates internal tensions and in-fighting that prevent unity against oppression.

Even as Asian Americans share some experiences of racism within the United States, we must be careful not to gloss over differences across Asian American communities and experiences. While Asian Americans can work together in solidarity to combat racist oppression, the differences among Asian cultures that still inform many Asian American individuals and communities are also significant. That means Asian American feminist theologians work out of both their own particular cultures (Korean, Hmong, Chinese, Indian, etc.), and they work out of an awareness of the hybridized Asian American identities fostered by the unique position of people with Asian ancestry in the United States. As feminist theologian Kwok Pui-lan notes, "Asian feminist theologians should guard against presenting a monolithic, simplified notion of what it means to be 'Asian'" (Kwok 2000, 41).

In the United States, Asian Americans are often racialized as foreigners by the center. Asian Americans are the only group of people of color who are viewed as perpetual foreigners. One of the earliest immigrants to the continental United States was the Filipinos who arrived on October 18, 1587, from the Philippines. Even though Asian Americans have been here in the United States for over 500 years, there is a negative perception that Asian Americans cannot be "real" Americans. This fuels the narrative that Asian Americans will continuously be viewed as foreigners in the land where they were born.

One of the grave consequences, for example, of the idea of Asian Americans as perpetual foreigners happened during World War II. The US government relocated many Japanese Americans, especially in the West, and put them into internment camps. These Japanese Americans who had lived on American soil for many generations lost everything, their homes, lands, and belongings, and faced deplorable conditions in the internment camps. Many Japanese American women suffered immensely during the internment as they gave birth and took care of their babies in the camps. At the same time, America was at war with other countries like Germany, but no Germans were arrested and put into internment camps. Only Japanese people were rounded up and put into camps. This resulted from the negative view that Asian Americans are perpetual foreigners and during times of war are not and cannot be viewed as Americans. They were foreigners who might have brought harm and danger to the United States in wartime.

Marginality

We are accustomed to thinking from the central perspective and believe that the center defines the margin. In the United States, white people are at the center, and Asian Americans are on the margins; men are at the center, and women are on the margins. The margin is receptive and reacts to what happens at the center. In this way, Asian Americans and particularly Asian American women react to whatever happens in the center. Within the dominant culture, they do not define who they are, but rather, they get defined by those in the center. For example, Asians have been defined racially as "yellow" by dominant white culture, even though they are not yellow. Asian American women are subsumed under the term "women of color," even though Asian American women did not create that term for themselves.

From the perspective of centrality, ethnic minorities are marginal people who live in between two cultures. Being in-between means belonging to neither. They are alienated not only from the dominant world but from themselves, which pulls them toward two different identities and eventually deprives them of an integrated self-image of themselves. The norm of marginality moves from the center to the boundaries of society. This movement in marginality is historically inevitable as cultures are dynamic and not static. As cultures change and modify, so does the understanding of marginality and who actually exists in the margins.

Marginality means being at the border that connects the two worlds that the marginalized belong to: their own culture as well as the dominant white culture. That is why those in the margins exist between the two cultures. These margins are complicated by intersections of gender, sexuality, class, and other forms of social difference, so that margins and relationships to the center are always fluid and in motion. For example, women who work in predominantly male occupations (like theology) occupy and exist in-between two worlds: the patriarchal world of men and the world of traditional women who may resent their more liberated sisters. These women in non-traditional occupations are alienated from the two worlds without wholly belonging to either of them. Asian American women are doubly marginalized in the workforce not only because of gender but also because of race and ethnicity. We see this in the ways Asian American women are de facto segregated into certain occupations and in the ways that, when women are allowed access to non-traditional occupations, white women are most likely to attain these positions.

The marginal experience is affected by intersections of gender with race, ethnicity, social class, sexuality, ability, immigration status, nation of origin, politics, education, occupation, religion, and age. These factors are interdependent and have significant shaping influence on each other (Lee, 33). The determinants of margin and center are also interwoven and interrelated. The center is powerful as it defines the implied standards from which all others who are different can be declared to deviate and be understood as imperfect. Furthermore, while that ideal and centrality is perpetuated by those whose interests it serves, it can also be internalized by those who are oppressed by it which can lead to dangerous consequences (Ferguson 1990, 9).

The spaces in the margins, however, can also be sites of creativity and power, and it is within these spaces that Asian American feminist theologians operate. The margins are spaces to erase the distinction between colonizer and colonized, master and slave. The margins, in a sense, become a powerful site of resistance to the center (Bhabha 1990, 343). This site of creativity is a place where we recognize that marginalized voices can be heard, acknowledged, and celebrated. Women in the margins can really celebrate and do the things that they have been pushed out of doing in the center. From the margins, Asian American feminist theologians have been able to develop theologies that both name and critique oppression and also offer hope, resistance, and resilience.

In this space of oppression, Asian American women's liberation and empowerment also arose. Despite being silenced, marginalized, and rendered invisible by both racial and gendered structures, Asian American women were able to find some strength in their shared experiences. Through their shared experience of marginality, they were not only able to survive but were also able to be transformed. Power emerged out of pain, and a prophetic voice emerged from silence.

INVISIBILITY AND HYPERVISIBILITY

Because racism is talked about in binary terms in the United States, most Americans understand racism as a black and white dichotomy. The people who do not fit into this dichotomy are often ignored, and their experiences of racial bias and discrimination are not seen as racism. The denial of racist experience brings much pain and anguish to Asian Americans who have to deal with racism constantly. Their communities' long history of racism, prejudice, and oppression are diminished, and their own experiences of pain and suffering are rendered invisible. There is a disconnect between their lived experiences of oppression and the perceived perception by other people that Asian Americans are doing great and must not be suffering since they are "model minorities."

This invisibility minimizes the oppression and suffering of Asian Americans, especially Asian American women who are doubly invisible. Their issues are not taken seriously in the dominant society nor their own Asian American communities. At the same time, Asian American women are hyper invisible because of the Western (white) standards of beauty that deem Asian features less desirable and a marker of sexual availability and submissiveness.

This has resulted in a kind of self-hatred among many Asian women who cannot measure up to the Western standard of beauty. The dominant white beauty norm causes many Asian women to feel ashamed of the way they look. Plastic surgery then becomes a tempting option for some of these women in their quest to look more Western and be more acceptable in either their own or Western culture. In other words, many Asian women have internalized the white standard of beauty in part because they have rarely seen a person of color depicted as having innate beauty. In the United States, young Asian American girls are often encouraged to look less Asian and more Western. They dream of having bigger, rounder eyes, high-bridge pointed noses, and larger breasts, all in all, to look less Asian. They use make-up to make shadows on their face to make their noses look pointier than they actually are. Some young girls put tape on their eyelids to create the double eyelid, which is such a desirable Western feature among young Asian American women.

In many Asian cultures, women's bodies are often viewed with suspicion and even disgust. Nantawan Boonprasat Lewis contends that internalizing negative images can make women feel helpless and lead them to become "willing victims." She says instead Asian women should develop self-definition, self-rehabilitation, and self-acceptance (Lewis 1995, 228–229). In the United States, Asian American feminist theologians have decried the Western beauty norm as an affront to the inherent and God-given worth of Asian American women. Many Asian women in the United States and abroad have internalized Western beauty standards. So, for example, the number of facial reconstructions in Korea has skyrocketed, and Korea is now the number one place to do facial reconstruction. Many Asian women desire white women's features such as large eyes, bigger noses, and chiseled jaw lines. Some Asian American feminist theologians are speaking out on this issue as it goes against the inherent beauty of everyone, as we are all created in the image of God.

Out of such history, background, and context have emerged important reflections, narratives, and theology from Asian American women's lives. The distinct voices of Asian American women who have struggled and persevered through their religious and theological journeys are important to hear and examine. Experiences of immigration, marginalization, racism, sexism, and adaptation of their bi-religious heritages mark their history. Kwok Pui Lan's contributions to postcolonial Asian feminist theology provide essential frameworks for reinterpreting scripture and examining the oppression experienced by Asian women under colonial rule. Through her postcolonial lens, she uncovers the deep-rooted patterns of subordination and othering that colonialism inscribes on women's identities and experiences. In a similar vein, Rita Nakashima Brock has critically addressed violence against women within the context of Christian theology. Her examination of atonement theory reveals how traditional, male-centered interpretations can perpetuate harm against women and children. Brock's feminist theology disrupts these dominant narratives, offering life-giving alternatives that prioritize healing, justice, and the dignity of the oppressed.

As we study the past of Asian American women, it gives us a good backdrop to our present context and how identity, spirituality and gender roles are shaped and formed for them. A theology of visibility counters the experiences of many

Asian American women who are made invisible not only by dominant white society but also by Asian American culture.

SYNCRETISM AND INTERFAITH DIALOGUE

Unique to Asian American feminist theologies of liberation is the importance of syncretism and interfaith dialogue. Asians have a rich and longstanding history of spirituality and religious traditions. Asian American women often draw from this deep heritage as they engage in interfaith dialogue and navigate their own theological journeys. Theologians like Kwok Pui Lan and Chung Hyun Kyung emphasize the importance of syncretism through the blending of religious traditions as a meaningful and necessary part of theological reflection. They advocate for ongoing interfaith engagement as a way to honor the complexity of spiritual identities, challenge exclusivist frameworks, and cultivate more inclusive and dynamic expressions of faith. As Asian American women dig deep into their own religious and spiritual heritage, which they have inherited from their mothers and grandmothers and their ancestors, they are developing their own feminist theological imaginations and movements for liberation.

Kwok Pui Lan emphasizes the importance of multifaith hermeneutics as a valuable approach to reading and interpreting the Bible. This method draws on texts, insights, and traditions from multiple religious faiths to foster deeper understanding and meaningful dialogue. Asia is the birthplace of all the world's major religions. Thus, Asian American women have inherited this rich religious past. This is helpful in their own theological journey as they can incorporate multifaith hermeneutics in their biblical reading as well as in feminist theological discourse. By examining both shared and distinct perspectives across faith traditions, multifaith hermeneutics opens up new interpretive possibilities and challenges narrow, single-lens readings of scripture. This approach not only enriches biblical interpretation but also promotes a more holistic and inclusive understanding of the sacred, one that would otherwise remain limited without such interreligious engagement.

THEOLOGY OF VISIBILITY

Out of Asian American women's experiences of invisibility and the denial of their experiences of racism, Grace Ji-Sun Kim has developed a theology of visibility. A theology of visibility raises issues of marginalization and liberation using four Korean words and concepts: *ou-ri, han, Jeong,* and *chi. Ou-ri,* meaning "our," captures a collective sense of Asian experience; *han,* meaning "unjust suffering," describes the overwhelming feeling of despair that results from unresolved injustice; *jeong* is "sticky love," the unconditional love that keeps relationships together; and *Chi,* an Asian concept that signifies the spirit. These concepts help define Asian society by organizing the collective sense of self and shared group identity, which contradicts the ideals of Western society. For Asian American women to become visible as full participants in the kin-dom of God, theology must embrace these Asian concepts and make them part of the theological conversation (Kim 2021, 139).

Ou-ri

Community overrides individualism in Asian society, and this commitment is imbued directly into the language of Asian societies. This language solidifies how one perceives the world and how it impacts their actions and behaviors. The Korean language uses the term *ou-ri,* a possessive plural that means "our" to talk about what the West would use the possessive singular, "my." In Korea, people do say not "my mother" but rather "our mother," even in families with just one child, as there is a sense of community or a larger family. Plural possessive pronouns are also used for other possessions, such as "our house," not "my house." Even when someone is referring to their own spouse, they say, not "my spouse," but "our spouse" even though they are only married to one person (Kim 2021, 140). This is how Korean grammar creates, communicates, and maintains community, in contrast with the individualism of the West.

The use of the plural possessive noun may seem like a small and insignificant factor in how one does theology, but it does alter our ways of thinking and imagining. Using the plural possessive noun like it is used in Korea, even for singular possessives, shifts how one views oneself, others, creation, and God. The plural possessive moves us away from focusing on ourselves and toward the greater collective and community. It forces us to look at community, the body of Christ, and the communion of saints as elemental forces that exist harmoniously outside Western individualism. Taking on a widened perspective, the Korean concept of plural possessive nouns pushes us to consider not only ourselves, care not only for ourselves, and regard not only ourselves but also the larger community and all of creation. (Kim 2021, 139) It becomes a helpful concept when trying to move toward a theology of visibility that wants to uplift Asian American women because they are important members of a community that values the community over the individual.

Han

Koreans have a word to express painful suffering, described as a piercing of the heart. This type of pain comes from unjust misery. When there are systems set up to cause suffering, then *han* is experienced. *Han* is caused by racism, colonialism, slavery, and sexism, which establish the subordination, exploitation, and oppression of groups of people. The suffering is amplified by the gravity of the circumstances and the feeling of being unable to escape the evil systems that cause *han* (Kim 2021, 140). Many Asian American women's experiences of racism and sexism lead to a tremendous amount of *han*. The effect of invisibility on Asian American women contributes to their experiences of *han*.

Han causes a deep wound in one's heart, and if one cannot find a source of healing, it is believed that the pain is carried on to death or is the cause of one's death. Thus, *han* can be passed from one generation to the next as unresolved feelings of sorrow, grief, and suffering can linger on for decades, affecting the victim's descendants. *Han* can be experienced individually or collectively. *Han* forces us to recognize the pain and suffering that occurs as a result of evil human constructs. It reminds us that sin isn't just a vertical event against God; it is also a horizontal one against our neighbors. Theology needs to deal with the circumstances, including social structures, that cause us to sin against others and work toward some form of liberation from the devastating pain of *han*. Asian American women are wounded due to racism, discrimination, patriarchy, and sexism from both white society and Asian American culture. A theology of visibility can decenter white male Eurotheology that contributes to invisibility and help lift Asian American women out of their pain and suffering (Kim 2021, 143, 144). The task of Asian American feminist theology is to release the crippling experiences of *han* so that Asian American women can be liberated from *han* and flourish.

Jeong

Jeong permeates the lives of Koreans; it is part of what gives joy and meaning to many people's lives. *Jeong* is a difficult word to translate into English, but it can be understood as love which encompasses a meaning that is greater and vaster than love, including affection, attachment, compassion, kindness, sharing, connection, and sympathy toward people and objects. *Jeong* captures the essence of love and affection between people that is sticky, like honey on our fingertips. This sticky kind of love is difficult to separate or untangle oneself from and makes us stay connected to one another. There is also a sense of collectiveness or community, as *jeong* diminishes the "I" and the boundaries attached to it and blurs the distinctions between people. The experience of collectiveness is common in Asia, which keeps people accountable to one another. It is largely absent in the Western world but could be something Westerners accept and enact, rather than the usual comparative acknowledgment, and even learn from. *Jeong* is understood as a bond between people. It is a love that keeps people together even in the midst of pain, suffering and *han*. It is an unconditional bond between friends and family that is not dependent on one's actions but present because of the relationship that exists (Kim 2021, 144, 145). *Jeong* is like the string that ties the communities together amidst all its differences; it can bring people together and keep them bound together which is so important for us today living in a broken world.

CHI

Spirit, or the Holy Spirit, is expressed in more than one language in the Bible—in Hebrew in the First Testament as *ruach* and in Greek as *pneuma* in the Christian Testament. As theology becomes global, our language must evolve to integrate words from other cultures. These other languages and ways of life are crucial to expanding our understanding of God and move us toward a universal theological discourse. Asian American feminist theologians encourage us to use Asian words and concepts in Christian theology to help us all get a better understanding of the mystery of the divine. *Chi* is an Asian concept similar to the biblical words *ruach* and *pneuma*. *Chi* means "wind," "energy," and "breath," but it gives a more embodied sense of the Spirit, which is sometimes lost in contemporary Western understandings of "spirit."

In the Western world, the body tends to be seen as separate from Spirit, and in white Eurocentric Christianity, the Holy Spirit is sometimes portrayed as a disembodied, abstract concept. Chi helps us understand that the Spirit lives in us and is a part of our selves (Kim 2011, 5). The Holy Spirit viewed as *Chi* is a helpful way to talk about the Spirit of God as it helps people experience God as an embodied God who is within them. The Spirit of God is not something that exists out there in the universe and is separate from our very own existence. It is part of humans who encourages us, sustains us, and comforts people. *Chi* intertwines with *jeong* to bring us together with each other to create a loving community which emphasizes *ou-ri* over the individual. This is the act of *Chi* who resides within us to give us light, energy, power, and life.

The Spirit as *Chi* helps us come to terms with an embodied sense of the Spirit and not a spirit which exists out in the universe. *Chi* is what gives us life and when we die, the *Chi* leaves our bodies making our bodies cold. *Chi* is the powerful movement of the Spirit which is felt among Asian American women that empowers them and gives them the energy to work harder for justice.

VISIBILITY IN THE KIN-DOM OF GOD

Asian American women's concerns are not heard, and their stories of racism and sexism are not prioritized, even in Asian American culture. In the theological world, Asian American feminist theologians argue that invisibility has no place in the kin-dom of God as the kin-dom of God embraces all people and values each person. The kin-dom of God does not erase people's names or eliminate groups of people but instead creates a banquet where all are welcome to the feast. Asian American women bear the image of God like all people, yet they continue to be marginalized, subjugated, oppressed, and made invisible by the church. Even as white feminists challenged the church, Asian American women's concerns were rarely included in the theological conversation. Even in feminist spaces, they were still invisible.

Invisibility as a theological concept needs to be taken seriously and be viewed as a spiritual issue. It affects how people view and understand God and God's creation and how people treat one another in this global world (Kim 2021, 150). Recognizing what is happening to Asian American women, a theology of visibility should encourage others to be in solidarity with Asian American women.

Bringing to light the struggles of Asian American women is the beginning point of doing a theology of visibility. It makes visible the pain and suffering of Asian American women that have been systematically and continuously diminished and hidden from society and the church. As Asian American women continue to fight for justice and seek a place at the theological table, a theology of visibility becomes a flourishing method of theology. It takes serious consideration of their ethnic culture and heritage and moves forward toward a theology of liberation and empowerment.

QUEER ASIAN AMERICAN THEOLOGIES

Perhaps even more invisible than Asian American women have been queer Asian Americans. Despite their long presence in the United States and in Asian cultures, queer Asians have been overlooked, ignored, and silenced. In the 1970s and 1980s, queer Asian Americans began to organize and form associations and collectives for support and activism. In the 1990s, queer Asian American theologians began to write about the LGBTQI+ Asian American experience.

Queer Asian American theologian Patrick Cheng suggests these writings can be organized into three thematic strands: "(1) Asian and Asian American church exclusion; (2) critiquing LGBTIQ racism; and (3) highlighting transnational perspectives" (Cheng 2013, 39). Leng Lim wrote some of the earliest essays that critiqued the exclusion of queer people from Asian and Asian American churches. In "The Gay Erotics of My Stuttering Mother Tongue" (Lim 2012, 172–177), Lim talks about the experience of growing up gay in Singapore and the ways his native tongue did not give him a language to talk about his sexuality. Lim has also written about the pain caused by the church for queer Asian Americans and has criticized church leaders who do not accept queer people. The second theme Cheng elaborates is a critique of the racism of the white queer community. Even in queer spaces, Asian American and other queers of color can experience racism when dominant white community members are not actively anti-racist. Cheng points out that failing to pay attention to intersectionality is the "sin of singularity"—not addressing both racism and homophobia (Cheng 2013, 39). Finally, Cheng notes the theme of transnational perspectives in queer Asian American theologies. These theologies recognize that the lines between nations, cultures, immigration, and migration, domestic and international, are often blurred, and these borders need to be crossed in liberatory theologies.

BIBLIOGRAPHY

Anderson, Kay J. 1999. *Vancouver's Chinatown: Racial Discourse in Canada, 1875-1980*. McGill-Queen's University Press.

Bhabha, Homi K. 1990. "The Other Question: Difference, Discrimination and the Discourse of Colonialism," p. 71–88. In *Out There: Marginalization and Contemporary Cultures*, Eds. Russell Ferguson, Martha Gever, Trinh T Minh-ha & Cornel West: The New Museum of Contemporary Art.

Chan, Sucheng. 1991. *Asian Americans: An Interpretive History*. Twayne Publishers.

Cheng, Patrick. 2013. *Rainbow Theology: Bridging Race, Sexuality, and Spirit*. Seabury: Seabury.

Cheng, Patrick. 2012. *From Sin to Amazing Grace: Discovering the Queer Christ*. Seabury.

Fernandez, Eleazar S., Eleazar. 2003. "American from the Hearts of a Diasporized People," In *Realizing the America of Our Hearts: Theological Voices of Asian Americans*, Eds. Fumitaka Matsuoka & Eleazar S. Fernandez. Chalice Press.

Ferguson, Russell. 1990. "Introduction: Invisible Center," p. 9–18. In Foreword by Marcia Tucker. *Out There: Marginalization and Contemporary Cultures*, Eds. Russell Ferguson, Martha Gever, Trinh T. Minh-ha & Cornel West. The New Museum of Contemporary Art.

Ho, Tamara C. 2019. "The Complex Heterogeneity of Asian American Identity," p. 17–26. In *T&T Clark Handbook of Asian American Biblical Hermeneutics*, Eds. Yang Seung Ai & Kim. Uriah. Bloomsbury/T&T Clark.

Kim, Grace Ji-Sun. 2003. *The Grace of Sophia: A Korean North American Women's Christology*. Pilgrim Press.

Kim, Grace Ji-Sun. 2011. *Holy Spirit, Chi and the Other*. Palgrave MacMillan.

Kim, Grace Ji-Sun. 2021. *Invisible: Theology and the Experience of Asian American Women*. Fortress.

Kwok, Pui-lan. 2000. *Introducing Asian Feminist Theology*. Pilgrim Press.

Lewis, Nantawan Boonprasat et al. 1995. "Toward an Ethic of Feminist Liberation and Empowerment: A Case Study of Prostitution in Thailand," p. 219–230. In *Christian Ethics in Ecumenical Context*, Ed. Shin Chiba. Eerdmans.

Lee, Mary Paik. 1990. *Quiet Odyssey: A Pioneer Korean Woman in America*. Edited with an Introduction by Sucheng Chan. University of Washington Press.

Lim, Leng Leroy. 2012. "The Gay Erotics of My Stuttering Mother Tongue." Amerasia Journal, 22 (1): 172–177.

Matsuoka, Fumitaka. 1998. *The Color of Faith: Building Community in a Multiracial Society*. United Church Press.

Okihiro, Gary Y. 1994. *Margins and Mainstreams: Asians in American History and Culture*. University of Washington Press.

Takaki, Ronald. 1989. *Strangers From a Different Shore: A History of Asian Americans*. Little, Brown and Company.

WOMANIST THEOLOGIES

Womanist theologies begin in the experiences of Black women. Drawing on a history of Black women's survival through enslavement, Jim Crow segregation, disenfranchisement, discrimination, and gendered and racialized violence at the hands of both white and Black men, Womanist theologies offer important insights into theological questions from the perspectives of women who are multiply marginalized. Black women contend white women can not speak for them as their experiences of being and becoming women, shaped by race, are vastly different from those of white women. Black women have experienced the long legacy of gendered and racialized oppression, which have impacted their lives and livelihoods. Because their long history of oppression at the intersection of gender and race is so different from white women's experience of sexism, Black women need their theological voice to counter the negative effects of sexism and racism in society and sexism within the black church and Christian theology.

Womanist theology challenges the omissions of much of white feminist theologies that often overlook or ignore race and class as crucial factors in an inclusive theology. These theologies first emerged, not in the academy, but in the lives of ordinary Black women reflecting on their experiences in light of their faith. Womanist theologian Eboni Marshall Turman argues that long before Womanist theological discourse entered the academy, "it was flourishing in the faithful lives of black Christian women. Womanism was born around black women's kitchen tables, on front porches, in beauty shops, in women's clubs, in the varieties of black women's prayer closets, and in various 'women's spaces' within the black church" (2019, 30). It is the lived experiences of Black women which are crucial in the development of a Womanist theology that will be liberating and empowering for Black women.

In her book, *In Search of Our Mothers' Gardens: Womanist Prose*, Alice Walker (1983) defined a womanist as "black feminist or feminist of color" who loves other women and/or men sexually and/or non-sexually, appreciates women's culture and strength, and is committed to the survival of all people. Black women do not live in isolation but in the larger white, dominant society. For them to survive means a survival for other women. Womanist theologian Katie Cannon (1995) calls womanism a "benchmark event" that has provided Black women a key way to challenge racism and sexism within Black and white communities and to encourage resistance through "revolutionary acts of rebellion."

Womanist theologies, like Asian American feminist theologies, lie at the intersection of racism and sexism, which work together to oppress Black women in particular ways. For example, Black women have not been treated with the same dignity as white women and have been subjected to racialized gender violence. Womanist theology arises from this lived reality that recognizes that Black women's experiences are distinct and cannot be fully understood through the lens of either racism or sexism alone.

Womanist theologians reveal the intersecting injustices of racism and sexism not as abstract concepts, but as lived realities that deeply affect Black women. Womanist theologians seek to name these injustices clearly and try to resist and transform them through a liberative theological lens. Womanist theologies are rooted in Black women's survival and struggle, which becomes a testament to the enduring strength and resilience of Black women. Womanist theologies are theologies that are grounded in truth-telling and justice and in the belief that survival is sacred, resistance is holy, and liberation is necessary.

According to feminist theologian Stephanie Y. Mitchem (2002), womanist theology is one of these revolutionary acts of rebellion. According to Mitchem, womanist theology begins in ethical analysis that responds to all forms of oppression (2002, 57). Echoing Black feminist Audre Lorde, Mitchem argues that the urgency of survival for all oppressed people means that womanist theologians cannot create hierarchies of oppression, ranking some oppressions as worse than others. Rather, all oppressions must be addressed simultaneously in order for real justice to be achieved.

Womanist theologian Delores Williams (n.d.) identifies four elements of womanist theological method: multidialogical intent, liturgical intent, didactic intent, and commitment to the validity of female imagery and metaphorical language. The multidialogical intent of womanist theology is "participation in dialogue and action with many diverse social, political, and religious communities concerned about human survival and productive quality of life for the oppressed." Liturgical intent calls for attention to and challenge of "the thought, worship, and action of the black church," requiring the church to develop and practice its liturgy with justice at the center. Didactic intent is the commitment to teach "new insights about moral life based on ethics supporting justice for women, survival, and a productive quality of life for poor women, children, and men." Womanist theology must also be open to content rooted in "female imagery, metaphor, and story." In doing so, womanist theology brings Black women's experiences and culture into the larger discourses of Christian theology as an instrument of social and theological change.

Womanist ethicist Emilie Townes (2003) enumerates the ways womanist theology has developed since finding its first formal expression in Katie Cannon's 1985 "The Emergence of Black Feminist Consciousness": "an orientation to Black women's survival in an oppressive social order that is classist, racist, and sexist; a framework for interpreting and critiquing the role of the Black Church; an interrogation of and critique of the Black Churches' appropriation of scripture in oppressive ways; a model for Black women's organizational strength; a critique of Black social stratification; advocacy for justice-based spirituality; the inclusion of ecological concerns; a concern for health care; a consideration of Black sexuality; and the issue of work."

The key task of Womanist theology is a reconsideration and reconstruction of Christian theology with Black women's lives at the center. Below, we outline how womanist theologians have engaged this task with some of the typical categories of Christian theology. These summaries represent some of the historic and contemporary ways womanist theologians have thought about God, Christology, redemption, and the church.

GOD IN WOMANIST THEOLOGIES

In Womanist theologies, as in process theologies, God is what God does. In other words, God is understood in terms of God's actions in the world on behalf of the survival of Black women. Delores Williams explains that for Black women, God is the one who "makes a way out of no way" (1993a, xi). This image comes from Black women's experiences of identifying God at work in their history, helping them to survive. Karen Baker-Fletcher calls this quality of God, "making do" (1997, 156–157). This, as Baker-Fletcher explains, is God's "sustaining activity" that ensures the survival of Black women. Monica Coleman describes this image as "an expression that acknowledges God's presence in providing options that do not appear to exist in the experiences of the past." It "acknowledges both the role of God and of human agency in new ways that break forth into the future" (2008, 33).

Kelly Brown Douglas identifies freedom as both a characteristic of God and the direction of God's action in the world on behalf of Black women. She writes of songs by enslaved Black women and men, as their proclamation that "their desire to be free was not only something God supported but something consistent with who God was. They were testifying to the very freedom of God" (Douglas 2015, 143). God's movement in history was testimony of God's freedom. Douglas adds that awareness of God's freedom empowered enslaved people to reject their enslavers, projections of

God—a white slave master on a throne keeping Black people in line—as an image that was not free. Rather, they embraced the freedom that was theirs before enslavement and the God they encountered there. They recognized that God was not with the enslavers but rather God was on the side of freedom because God is freedom.

All of this means that God continues to act with and on behalf of Black women toward freedom in their contemporary struggles at the intersections of racism, sexism, and classism. Pamela Lightsey complicates our understanding of Black women's oppression further by reminding us of the role of heterosexism and homophobia in the church and in Black lesbians' struggle to survive and thrive in freedom. Black lesbians do not only face the challenges of images of God in the form of their oppressors, but they must also contend with the idea of a God who hates them for who they are as queer people. Lightsey quotes writer Ta'Shia Asanti, "As an adolescent, I was taught the two most important things a budding Black lesbian should know about God: that God is White and Male and that God hates homosexuals" (2015, 38). Lightsey reminds us that Womanist theologies must also take into account the ways heterosexism has shaped discourses about God and who is deserving of God's freedom and way out of no way. In particular, she notes that readings of the Bible that condemn queer people are inconsistent with God's love and freedom and that the Bible is not God and cannot be elevated above God. She adds, "As queers, we declare that God cannot be limited. God is not finite. God is not determinate as are we as created beings." That means God cannot be subordinated to human interpretations of a text about God (Lightsey 2015, 46).

Exclusively male God language and discourse reinforce the notion that men are more fully created in the image of God than women. This careless and patriarchal theology has become the norm and has been promoted widely in the church throughout history. Most women and girls never have the opportunity to experience their gender as being associated with God because of the church's focus on God's maleness. Women and girls of color and LGBTQI+ people, especially, rarely have the opportunity to imagine God as someone like them. For those who have experienced God as female, black or brown, or queer, writes Wil Gafney, the experience "has been profoundly moving, rare, and even sometimes profoundly disturbing" (2011, xxix). Womanist theologians recognize how much diverse people need to see a God who is like them to affirm their personhood and empower their work for justice.

Black male theologians like James Cone have said God is Black but have rarely challenged the assumption of God's maleness. Womanist theologians offer a challenge to this assumption by appealing, not only to God's blackness but also to God's femaleness. Christena Cleveland suggests the image of God as the "Sacred Black Feminine." This Black Feminine is with and for Black women because she is a Black woman. This Sacred Black Feminine declares Black women as sacred (Cleveland 2022, 17), beautiful, and worthy. This is to counter the narrative that Black women are not created in the Divine image and are somehow sinful. Dominant white society and Black male dominance in the Black church do not typically value the sacredness of Black women, and so, for Black women, to be called sacred is liberating and empowering. The discourse, language, and imagery of Black women must change for society to change its views and narratives about Black women.

Cleveland believes the Black Feminine helps Black women in their quest for liberation. She writes, "She is the God who smashes the white patriarchy and empowers us all to join in Her liberating work. She is the God who has a special love for the most marginalized because She too has known marginalization. She is the God who cherishes our humanity and welcomes our fears, vulnerabilities, and imperfections" (Cleveland 2022, 17). Cleveland adamantly opposes a white male God who wages war on Black women's bodies and creates fear for many Black women. Black women endured enslavement under white people who preached to them that God was a white man. A white male God legitimized the horrors of enslavement and the ongoing assault on Black women's bodies. They endured the wrath of the enslavers as well as sexual assault from them. A white patriarchal God continues to legitimize such horrors against Black women's bodies and minds. Thus, a Black feminine God is necessary if any form of liberation is to be achieved for Black women.

BLACK WOMEN'S CHRIST

A white Jesus, which has been promoted within most of Christianity, is also problematic for Black women. Jesus, of course, was not white; he was a Palestinian Jew. Jesus was born in the Middle East and therefore had dark skin, dark hair, and dark eyes. Yet, as the church evolved in Europe, it constructed Jesus as a white European man who legitimizes the power of white men and white supremacy in society.

White people invented the white Christ to reinforce the status quo and allow white men to continue to dominate over people of color, especially Black women. One of white supremacy's most powerful myths is the idea of the white Christ who solved white people's moral and practical dilemmas. A white Christ revealed that God preferred white people over Black people (Cleveland 2022, 39). A white Christ allowed enslavement to flourish as the white church taught that white people could rule over Black people. A white Christ legitimized segregation, and, even now, a white Christ enables ongoing mistreatment of people of color. The white Christ has been used throughout the church's history as a tool to place God on the side of white oppressors and demand the subservience of people of color as God's will.

Womanist theologians have called for Christian theology to move away from this white Christ to a Black Jesus who cares for Black women and their experiences of oppression. Kelly Brown Douglas is quick to add that a black Christ is not only a Black man or a Black woman. Rather, she says, a Black Christ must encompass all of the intersections. She argues that for a Black Christ to be fully liberating, the image must be multidimensional, confronting all the oppressions that harm Black communities, including heterosexism (Douglas 1994, 99). Racism is harmful, hurtful, and non-Christ-like as Christ seeks to rid of racism and heterosexism. She agrees with Jacquelyn Grant (1989) that Christ is found in Black women's experiences but adds that "Christ is found where Black people, men as well as women, are struggling to bring the entire Black community to wholeness" (Douglas 1999, 109). In other words, while Christ may be a Black woman, Christ is not limited to Black women.

WOMANIST THEOLOGIES OF SIN, SUFFERING, AND SALVATION

Central to Womanist theologies are questions of suffering and salvation. Womanist theologian Jacquelyn Grant claims that sorrow and sadness are quintessential facets of Black women's lives (1995). Suffering under oppressive systems at the intersection of sexism, racism, classism, and heterosexism characterizes both Black women's histories and present realities, and Womanist theologies take the significance of both seriously. Within Womanist theologies, suffering is not a requirement but a reality of living under oppressive systems. It is not God's will that Black women suffer, and, in fact, Black women's suffering is the result of sin against Black women. Salvation is liberation from this suffering and freedom to live without the impositions of oppression. While many Black women of faith have looked toward freedom in a life beyond this one, Womanist theologies situate freedom in both God's and Black women's own present actions toward liberation. As Womanist theologian Shawn Copeland puts it, "Black women invite God to partner with them in the redemption of Black people" (1993, 124).

For Womanist theologians, "Suffering in itself is not salvific" (Mitchem 2002, 109). Rather, it is a starting place for Black women to think about relationships with God, humans, and the world. By beginning with Black women's experiences, and in particular their suffering, Womanist theologies reject traditional notions of sin and salvation. Sin and salvation are not simply individual experiences; they are also collective and structural. Social structures that constrain and harm Black women are sinful; in the Black church, when sexism intersects with race, the Black church's mistreatment of Black women is sinful. The suffering that comes from mistreatment is not redemptive but is the result of sin against Black women. It can be made useful, however, as Black women reflect on suffering to impel them toward liberatory action on behalf of Black women.

Christena Cleveland points out how Black women, in particular, are perceived as distant from God by virtue of the intersections of racism and sexism. The Jezebel stereotype has been particularly damaging for Black women, who the dominant culture has situated as inherently impure (Cleveland 2022, 43). These negative narratives about Black women need to be challenged and eliminated for Black women to experience freedom and liberty.

Anti-blackness and anti-woman sentiment are embedded in Christianity, and anti-blackness toward Black women is especially virulent. Kelly Brown Douglas states that anything that belittles, degrades, or betrays the sacred humanity of another is violent as it separates one from the ways of a just and loving God. Whiteness is an intrinsically violent and sinful construct because it separates people into socially constructed categories to maintain white dominance (Douglas 2015, 3). Much of traditional Christian theology has supported this construction with its images of a white male God and a white Jesus that continue to feed false narratives about Black women and push them to the bottom of the hierarchy as doubly marginalized people.

Mitchem argues that the journey toward salvation/liberation begins with Black women's self-care (2003 111). As Delores Williams noted, abuse of human bodies is inherently sinful because humans are created in God's image (1993b, 144). Abuse of Black women is embodied structurally in institutions such as law and healthcare and in harmful actions of individuals toward Black women that are rooted in structures such as rape culture and Christian notions of servanthood. Caring for oneself is, then, a revolutionary act that claims Black women's rights to selfhood and bodily autonomy in the face of systems of oppression.

This care for Black bodies and Black agency extends to the Black community. Part of liberatory action includes work toward the transformation of society as well as the self. Kelly Brown Douglas calls this action "moral participation" (2015, 223). Moral participation is the requisite action of faith. Douglas explains that through God's work in the world toward liberation God invites people to become partners with God in transforming the world. Moral participation, she explains, "is, in effect, bearing the memory of Jesus in the world" (2015, 224).

WOMANIST UNDERSTANDINGS OF THE CROSS

As Mitchem points out, "Jesus is present *in* the troubles" of Black women (2002, 107). While historically, many Black people framed Jesus as a co-sufferer, contemporary Womanists recognize that this image can actually contribute to Black women's suffering by suggesting suffering is redemptive. Still, it can be useful as it demonstrates Jesus' solidarity with the oppressed. Douglas explains, "The cross reflects the lengths that unscrupulous power will go to sustain itself" (Brown 2015, 180). The cross, then, is not the model for redemptive suffering but rather the image of refusal to use the weapons of a "culture of death." She adds, "... these weapons cannot become divine weapons ... God did not defeat the cross with weapons of death" (Douglas 2015, 183). Williams reminds us that Christians "cannot forget the cross, but neither can they glorify it" (1993a, 167). The cross stands as a stark symbol of state violence, suffering, and injustice, and it was an instrument of death used to silence and oppress. The cross reminds us of the pain and sacrifice of Christ, and it symbolizes solidarity with all who suffer today. Yet, to glorify the cross without pointing out its brutality is to distort its meaning, for it becomes not a symbol of liberation but of domination.

Douglas argues that the resurrection is what makes plain the "wrongness" of the cross. She adds, "What the resurrection points to, however, is not the meaning of Jesus' death, but of his life." The resurrection demonstrates that "crucifying realities do not have the last word" (2015, 188). The resurrection is a divine affirmation of the way Jesus' life, teachings, and solidarity with the marginalized. The resurrection reveals that God's ultimate concern is life as the resurrection shifts the focus from suffering as redemptive to the abundant, liberating, and transformative life of Jesus. In rising, Jesus proclaims that the forces of empire, violence, and death do not have the final word as life, love, and justice prevail. Resurrection invites us not to dwell on the cross but to live into hope and love from Christ.

The resurrection offers hope and confirms the life-affirming message of the Gospel for Black women. Salvation is not to be found in suffering but in working toward God's desire for freedom for all people. Black women can use their sense of self, agency, experiences, and faith to be partners with God in transforming themselves and society.

WOMANISM AND THE BLACK CHURCH

The Black church is vital to Black women as a community is needed for liberation to occur and to be felt. The Black church becomes a very important community for Black women to experience freedom and liberation that the Bible speaks about in the Exodus story. Cole Arthur Riley writes that there cannot be a promised land without a multitude. Some may believe that they can get there alone, and perhaps by some stroke of luck, one can even achieve it alone. However, the promise achieved alone can be devastated and ruined by loneliness as one drinks the milk and eats the honey alone (Riley 2022, 81). Therefore, a community is desperately needed to journey together and to rejoice together. The community in many cases is the church, but is not always solely the church, as faithful communities can be found outside the church.

Black women believe that God is not just present in the church but also in the streets (Riley 2022, 51). Therefore, the community that is needed for liberation cannot be limited solely to the church and the body of Christ found within the church walls. Black women do not believe that the presence of God is only experienced during worship and in the church building. Rather, God is experienced in the streets where riots, pain, and assaults are happening. The presence of God is with Black women, whether they are in the church or outside the church.

While many Black women have found comfort and community in the Black church, the Womanist Black Christ challenges sexism in the Black church. Womanist theologians recognize that while the Black church has often provided respite from racism, it has often reproduced sexism in its treatment of Black women. Douglas argues, in particular, that Womanist theologians must be in dialogue with ordinary Black folks in the church, and the Black church, especially Black churchwomen, must be the primary audience for Womanist theologies. She says that the Black church must make room for Womanist theologies, and this means Black men in the church must be invested in Black women (Douglas 1994, 113–116).

While Williams finds great hope in the Black church, she distinguishes it from African-American denominational churches. The Black church is the Black Christian community writ large that struggles for liberation. Denominational churches, she insists, are guilty of a host of sins against Black women: denying Black women equal opportunity in church leadership; collusion with social and political forces in the United States that oppress Black women; sexual exploitation of Black women; discouragement of Black women from fighting for their own liberation; failure to deal with problems impacting Black women, such as poverty, drug-addiction, and HIV/AIDS; homophobia; building of church edifices while so many Black people live in poverty; and failure to meet needs of Black prisoners (Williams 1993a, 207–209). Williams' hope for the Black church is in its participation in the liberation of all Black people through a transformative struggle against systems of oppression that leads to justice and freedom.

Part of the liberation of all Black people can happen if the church works to become an anti-racist church. Rev. Jacqui Lewis, who is a minister of the Middle Church in Manhattan, believes that anti-racism must be at the center of the church. This includes the practice of love and being a church in the spirit of *ubuntu*. *Ubuntu* comes from the African understanding that everyone is inextricably connected and therefore, whatever choices we make will impact our families, community, and the world (Lewis 2021, 162). If the Black church embodies *ubuntu*, then interconnectedness will be experienced, and it will encourage growth and love within the church.

Womanist theologians remind the Black church that liberation must be around gender as well as race. If Black women are not free, then justice is not present (Riley 2022, 123). The role of the Black church is to work for justice so that everyone can experience freedom. The Sacred Black Feminine is love, and the Black church needs to practice and embody this love for Black women.

Ubuntu imagines the oppressed and oppressor both present in the end—connected and interdependent. Desmond Tutu draws from Jesus to build his imagination of what *ubuntu* will look like. "Jesus says, 'And when I am lifted up from the Earth, I shall draw everyone to myself,' as he hangs from His cross without-flung arms, thrown out to clasp all, everyone and everything, in a cosmic embrace, so that all, everyone, everything, belongs" (Harper 2022, 215–216).

The Black church's liturgy, sermons, and biblical interpretation must help Black women and not contribute further to their subordination and oppression. Wil Gafney points out that "androcentrism, sexism, and misogyny in the scriptures, in their translation, and their preaching and liturgical use, hurts men and boys and nonbinary children and adults as much as it does women and girls" (2021, xxix). Gafney emphasizes rereading and reinterpreting scripture away from patriarchy, which has been destructive and damaging to Black women. As sites of liberation, the Black church should be a place where people see and hear Black and female images and language about God that are empowering for all people.

BIBLIOGRAPHY

Baker-Fletcher, Karen. 1997. *My Sister, My Brother: Womanist and Xodus God-Talk*. Orbis Books.

Cannon, Katie G. 1995. *Katie's Canon: Womanism and the Soul of the Black Community*. Continuum.

Coleman, Monica. 2008. *Making a Way Out of No Way: A Womanist Theology*. Fortress.

Copeland, M. Shawn. 1993. "Wading Through Many Sorrows: Toward a Theology of Suffering in Womanist Perspective," In *A Troubling in My Soul: Womanist Perspectives on Evil and Suffering*, Ed. Emilie M. Towns. Orbis Books.

Cleveland, Christena. 2022. *God Is a Black Woman*. HarperOne.

Douglas, Kelly Brown. 1994. *The Black Christ*. Orbis Books.

Douglas, Kelly Brown. 2015. *Stand Your Ground: Black Bodies and the Justice of God*. Orbis.

Gafney, Wilda C. 2021. *A Women's Lectionary for the Whole Church, Year A*. Church Publishing.

Grant, Jacquelyn. 1995. "Womanist Jesus and the Mutual Struggle for Liberation," In *The Recovery of Black Presence*, Eds. Randall C. Bailey & Jacquelyn Grant. Abingdon.

Grant, Jacquelyn. 1989. *White Women's Christ and Black Women's Jesus: Feminist Christology and Womanist Response*. Scholars Press.

Harper, Lisa Sharon. 2022. *Fortune: How Race Broke My Family and the World-And How to Repair It All*. Brazos Press.

Lewis, Jacqui. 2021. *Fierce Love: A Bold Path to Ferocious Courage and Rule-Breaking Kindness That Can Heal the World*. Harmony.

Lightsey, Pamela. 2015. *Our Lives Matter: A Womanist Queer Theology*. Pickwick.

Mitchem, Stephanie Y. 2002. *Introducing Womanist Theology*. Orbis Books.

Riley, Cole Arthur. 2022. *This Here Flesh: Spirituality, Liberation and the Stories That Make Us*. Convergent.

Townes, Emilie. M. 2003. "Womanist Theology." https://irbe.library.vanderbilt.edu/server/api/core/bitstreams/b2aab524-85e7-488d-9302-e9b3d4e55bb4/content. Accessed October 26, 2024.

Turman, Eboni Marshall. 2019. "Black Women's Wisdom." *The Christian Century*, 136 (6): 30–34.

Walker, Alice. 1983. *In Search of Our Mothers' Gardens: Womanist Prose*. Harcourt Brace Jovanovich.

Williams, Delores S. 1993a. *Sisters in the Wilderness: The Challenge of Womanist God-Talk*. Orbis Books.

Williams, Delores S. 1993b. "A Womanist Perspective on Sin," p. 130–149. In *A Troubling in My Soul: Womanist Perspectives on Evil and Suffering*, Ed. Emilie Townes.

Williams, Delores S. _____. n.d. "Womanist Theology: Black Women's Voices." https://www.religion-online.org/article/womanist-theology-black-womens-voices/. Accessed October 25, 2024.

ECOFEMINIST THEOLOGIES

Climate change is happening right before our eyes, and it is creating a lot of dangerous problems, havoc, and chaos on our planet Earth, especially for women in the developing world. Climate change is one of the most important justice issues of our time, as it is producing illness, climate refugees, destruction, and death across the globe. It is causing a lot of people to experience extreme difficulties due to the rise in temperature and the rise in sea levels, which are affecting poorer island countries as well as coastal cities that will be destroyed if we do not do anything about this climate injustice. Everyone is affected by climate change, but women are affected more and suffer graver consequences from climate change. Ecofeminist theologians have taken up the challenge to address this important social justice and explore how we can work together to change the course of destruction that we are headed toward.

CREATION

The Bible begins with a creation story and the story highlights some of the beauty, wonder, and excitement of the things that God created. In the creation story, God creates through speaking into being all the wondrous creatures of every kind that swim in the sea, fly through the air, and walk on Earth. The creation story includes the repetition of the phrase "of every kind," which points to the vast biodiversity of species that God calls forth and creates in the world.

DOI: 10.4324/9781032643939-5

Speaking directly and specifically to creation, God blesses them and gives them the charge to be fruitful and multiply. The story observes that God takes notice of the wonderful and beautiful creation, "And God saw that it was good." According to the biblical story, all of creation has its common origin in the overflowing generosity of the Creator who vivifies them and pronounces them very good (Genesis 1:21, 25) (Johnson 2024, 50, 51). All of creation was declared good, and God's blessing rests upon every part of it. The beauty and glory of God are revealed through the very act of creation, where divine intention and presence are made visible in the natural world.

From such a wonderous beginning of creation on Earth, as eco-feminist theologians note, we have come to a point in our history where we are facing the destruction of planet Earth if we do not drastically change our ways of living and daily behaviors. Some scientists warn that certain forms of environmental damage caused by human activity may already be irreversible, signaling the urgent need for transformative action and a deeper sense of ecological responsibility.

Our decisions and actions to benefit our selfish desires and economic growth are exploiting the Earth and directly impacting the climate. There are always grave consequences to our actions. If we devastate a forest, there will be less water to drink, or if we divert the course of a river, the local agriculture will not be the same and may even perish. We will gradually feel the traumatic effects of our intervention against nature, and the effects could be deadly. Brazilian ecofeminist Ivone Gebara explains, if we destroy bees, there is no flower pollination, and if we produce harmful chemicals, we cause lung disease and terrible problems on the rest of the Earth (Gebara 2017, 6). The consequences of our actions upon the Earth are great, and this reminds us of how the Earth is sensitive to our actions and reacts to how we treat the Earth. The Earth is a living organism and therefore will feel pain if we damage it or destroy parts of it.

For ecofeminist theologians, the creation story's ideal of a very good creation, in and of itself and apart from its utilitarian value for humans, points the way toward our own transformation of the environment from its ravaged present to a healed and whole future. Rather than seeing the Genesis story as a mandate for humans to dominate the Earth, they see it as a model for human caretaking of the Earth. Destroying the environment is counter to the goodness of creation and brings illness, suffering, and death.

Sin and *Han*

Han is a Korean word that captures the essence of "unjust suffering." Koreans have collectively suffered under colonialism, wars, and subjugation by superpowers. People can experience *han* individually or collectively. It is immense pain that cuts into the heart and causes deep and terrible suffering. People experience problems that can cause them consternation, such as not having the right color clothes that they may want or missing a bus that they need to catch or not having an umbrella on a rainy day. These types of experiences may cause some level of pain or annoyance, but they do not rise to the level of *han*. *Han* comes with systemic injustice; it is a result of intersecting systems of racism, sexism, classism, heterosexism, ableism, ageism, and nationalism, which oppress through bias, discrimination, and violence to cause immense suffering, which is difficult to escape. Ecowomanist theologian Melanie L. Harris demonstrates the importance of intersectional thinking in the development of a feminist ecotheology. She explains, "The approach links a social justice agenda with Earth justice, recognizing the similar logic of domination at work in parallel oppressions suffered by women and the Earth. That is, just as women of color have often survived multiple forms of oppression when confronting racism, classism, sexism, and heterosexism, androcentric attitudes devaluing the Earth and privileging (particular) humans over the Earth's well-being has resulted in the environmental crisis in which we all find ourselves" (2016, 6). Environmental degradation causes *han* because it creates unjust suffering through its differential impact on the planet and all of the planet's inhabitants.

Han is not just limited to human beings, as animals and nature can also experience *han*. South African professor Lily

Nortjé-Meyer (2022) makes the case that animals, women, and the Logos are "interconnected flesh." Animals and nature suffer from abusive treatment by humans, yet they cannot protest against it or escape it. They also suffer from human-caused environmental degradation. Nature itself cannot escape this horrible system, which continues to cause harm and destruction. Therefore, the Earth and its inhabitants groan from their pain, and *han* becomes their inexpressible pain at being maltreated. Creation was not meant to be subjected to human exploitation, but creation has been forced to serve human whims and has suffered pain in so many ways. Nature tries to cope with all the stress it receives but is unable to bear the stress anymore as it is collapsing, and this suffering is nature's *han* (Park 1993, 42). As nature and the Earth suffer from *han*, we must take this situation seriously as the Earth is giving us warning signs and nature is calling out for humans to do better.

The Earth is suffering and crying out in pain and agony due to humans' greed, exploitation, and destruction. Global warming and the depletion of the ozone layer is the Earth's *han*. The Earth has been oppressed and manipulated. If we are serious about ecology and saving the planet, we must understand nature's *han*. Trees, water, air, and soil have been destroyed against their will. Human actions that contradict the will of nature produce *han*, and nature groans under the weight of this oppression. The Bible conveys this idea of *han* of all creation (Romans 8:19-23), yet we ignore this plight. We dismiss the *han*-ridden cry of nature and animals and have been judged by them in the form of ecological disasters. Many human beings have embraced anthropocentrism and have rejected the importance of nature and animals. In order to achieve a holistic vision of creation, we need to work to dissolve the *han* of animals and nature (Park 1993, 43). The evils of globalization, imperialism, and consumerism work to create *han*, and thus we need to work toward eliminating it, by prioritizing our work on sustainability and climate justice. There needs to be a dismantling of the systems that cause unjust suffering if we are to live in a harmonious relationship with others and nature.

Humanity's treatment of the Earth is similar to patriarchal societies' treatment of women. Women's bodies are taken advantage of and oftentimes abused, assaulted, and even discarded. How women are treated is often correlated to how the Earth is treated. Both are viewed as feminine, and both are viewed as someone or something to be conquered. There is a sense of domination and destruction toward women, just as toward the Earth. As men assault women (and queer people who are also often feminized), we recognize that humanity also assaults the Earth and damages it. Eco-feminist theologies recognize these important connections between women and the Earth/nature and argue that environmental justice also requires gender and racial justice.

WOMEN AND CLIMATE

Women live in precarious political, economic, and social situations around the world. Around the globe, they are economically poorer than men. Many women survive in substandard living conditions and experience assault on their bodies through domestic violence, sexual assault, and war. Women's bodies are devalued, and women are subject to gender discrimination and violence. Ecofeminist Ivone Gebara states that even circumstances that are harmful to all people, such as war, forced emigration, and natural disasters, differentially impact women, creating greater suffering (Gebara 2017, 69, 70) for women. While patriarchy is a global system, its manifestations and effects on women are shaped by context and culture. We see this clearly in climate change in the ways women in the global south or highly impoverished areas in the developed world suffer in greater ways than men in those same areas. Often, the responsibilities of childbearing and childrearing exacerbate women's problems because they are not as able as men to move away from the consequences of environmental degradation. When there is a food shortage, women often neglect their own health to feed their children. In many parts of the world, women and girls are responsible for gathering firewood for the family. Climate change is forcing them to go farther and farther afield to find wood. This also increases their vulnerability to sexual assault as they travel greater distances. Also, when men in families are under greater stress, women are at a greater risk of domestic violence.

Women's responses to these challenges vary. Some accept their suffering silently; others fight back and organize. For example, if there is a lack of drinking water, some may accept this situation as God's will, but some may organize the construction of wells. If there is an exposure to pesticides, some may ignore the risks, while others may refuse to consume any food containing pesticides. Women struggle to have clean water and food for their families, but generally, most decisions regarding the destruction of a forest, the diversion of a river, or the release of pollutants into the air are made by men. Men usually make decisions that affect the climate and women. (Gebara 2017, 69, 70). As men make these drastic and consequential decisions about the Earth, women live with the consequences of these actions. Some of these decisions are lifelong and life-threatening. Ecofeminist theologians see these actions as threats for generations to come. They contend that we must tackle climate change with the greatest urgency and do whatever we can to change the trajectory of our planet.

Oceania is facing climate change in drastic ways, as the Pacific region is a hot spot for climate change. Oceania eco-feminist theologian Seforosa Carroll paints a picture of how indigenous people have had a holistic and relational worldview of their relationship with their environment. They have intrinsically interconnected with the land, the sea, creation, and community, for the land (*vanua*, *fenua*, *whenua*), encompasses and embodies the physical, spiritual, social, and cultural (Carroll 2022, 410, 411). Their connection to the land has been disrupted by colonialism and Christian missions, and women are suffering greatly due to this disruption.

Oceania is diverse culturally, but generally a woman's position was dependent on her rank rather than on her gender. But under colonialism and Christianity, patriarchal systems were brought that removed women's power even in matrilineal structures. It shifted how women were viewed and the gender roles for women. With this change came the subordination of women, which results in a greater impact on women in this era of the climate crisis.

Many Christians have used the biblical creation story to justify the subordination of women and nature. Both, they argue, exist to serve men. Patriarchal theologies have drawn on women's close ties to nature through their association with the body (as opposed to men's association with mind/spirit) to rationalize men's dominance over women and the Earth. Ecofeminist theologians challenge these patriarchal theological notions by offering alternative understandings of God that support sustainability and women's equality.

For women in Oceania, this biblical Genesis story has created problems for how they tackle climate change, which is affecting their islands and homes. As colonialism and Christianity spread in the Pacific islander region, their indigenous worldviews were subjugated in favor of the new Christian spirituality. Sefora Carroll believes that Christian theology endorsed a dualistic worldview and silenced Indigenous views, which valued the relationship between people and the land. The Genesis creation story as interpreted by colonial forces portrayed the privileges of human beings as having full authority and dominion over creation, which was at odds with their indigenous beliefs of the interrelated, interdependent interconnectedness between humans and creation (Carroll 2022, 411).

This Genesis interpretation stands in stark contrast to Indigenous cosmologies. This theological framework disrupted Indigenous beliefs, devalued their spiritual insights, and contributed to some of the ecological disconnection. The consequences of Christian biblical teachings and misinterpretations have impacted the traditional beliefs and affected how women are viewed in relation to creation. Reclaiming and honoring these Indigenous perspectives is essential for restoring a more just, relational, and sustainable theology of creation.

Additionally, Christian missions taught the people of Oceania a personalized/individualized and spiritualized understanding of salvation and redemption. This has slowed down the actions of Pacific Islanders in fighting climate change. Carroll believes that it manifested in a passive faith which believes that "God will save us" and that all that is required is "to faithfully wait" (Carroll 2022, 411). This is highly problematic as human beings are responsible for our actions and what we do against nature. We cannot ignore our responsibility of creating this climate crisis and must engage in climate justice work.

QUEER/TRANS AND CLIMATE CHANGE

Not surprisingly, as subordinated people within heteropatriarchy, queer and trans people are also at greater risk for adverse impacts of climate change. For example, in the United States, queer and trans youth are more likely to become unhoused than any other group, and, of course, this vulnerability is shaped by race, ability, and social class, as well as gender and sexuality. Housing support is limited as it is, but, when severe weather hits, unhoused queer and trans youth have even fewer options for safety and support. Globally, climate change is also causing incredible displacement, forcing people, including queer and trans people, to become migrants or climate refugees. Many of the hardest hit areas also criminalize queerness, exacerbating risks to queer and trans people forced to move into camps or new areas. Queer and trans people also face additional barriers in applying for asylum or immigration. Gay men around the world and straight women in the global south are at greater risk of contracting HIV. Environmental pollutants can increase risk of pneumocystis pneumonia hospitalization in people who are HIV-positive. LGBTQI+ people also experience barriers and discrimination in accessing medical care. That means when queer and trans people's health is affected by the climate crisis, they may not seek or be able to attain appropriate healthcare.

Behind a great deal of worldwide discrimination against queer and trans people are theologies that suggest queer and trans identities are sinful. These theologies justify incredible injustice toward queer and trans people that is amplified by the climate crisis as queer and trans people are at greater risk of facing adverse consequences and being unable to access needed support. Ecofeminist theologies recognize the intersections of climate justice and justice for queer and trans people.

A queer ecofeminist theology recognizes that a binary analysis of the problems of climate change is inadequate to address the complexities of gender. It also disrupts the patriarchal association of woman with nature that underlies patriarchy by problematizing the nature of "woman" itself. Queer ecofeminism constructs nature, not as a passive object, but rather as an active and relational entity in which all entities participate. Queer scholar Daniel T. Spencer suggests an ethical shift, from "an anthropocentric, human-centered worldview" to an "ecocentric, all-of-life centered worldview" (2018, 16) grounded in queer desire that reclaims *eros* as the lifeforce that permeates and animates the relationships among all entities of the natural world. Jacob J. Erickson notes that many Christians suggest queerness is "unnatural." Instead, he suggests that nature itself is indeterminate, animated, vibrant, and constantly changing—a drag performance (2018, 74). Rather than seeing queer as unnatural, queer theologians see nature as queer. Whitney A. Bauman suggests that from queer perspectives, LGBTQI+ theologians can offer a new environmental ethic that reconnects humans to the planet and all of its inhabitants (2018, 113).

ECOFEMINIST THEOLOGIES AND METAPHORS FOR GOD

The Bible contains many parables and metaphors that convey the authors' understanding of who God is and God's message to humanity. Parables are stories that set the familiar in an unfamiliar context. A metaphor is a comparison that is often used in an unfamiliar context to give us new insights into a concept. Good metaphors challenge us to see the world in a different way (TeSelle 1975, 4). Theologians use metaphors to help us understand who God is and God's presence in this world. Common church metaphors include Father, Lord, and King, which convey and reinforce a patriarchal, masculine

God. For thousands of years, these masculine metaphors have perpetuated a patriarchal understanding of God that has had devastating consequences for women, queer and trans people, and the environment. They have taught us that men are more godlike and hence have justification for dominance over women, feminized others, and the Earth.

US Ecofeminist theologian Sallie McFague used different metaphors to speak about God and to discuss the horrific consequences of climate change. For her, metaphors are a way of knowing, not just a way of communicating. In metaphor, the knowledge and its expression are the same, and metaphors are expandable and flexible. Some may argue that some metaphors are inaccurate or misappropriate, but, rather, metaphors are necessary to speak about realities that transcend descriptive language (TeSelle 1975, 4). For ecofeminist theologians, metaphors are a helpful tool to speak about God in ways that move us toward climate justice and sustainability.

Some in the church confuse metaphors for the real things. Thus, if we use the metaphors of King, Master, and Lord, many in the church believe that God is an actual king, master, and lord. The consequences of such metaphors and beliefs allow and reinforce colonialism, imperialism, and domination of the Earth to occur. This is why we must remind ourselves that metaphor helps point to God but is not God. Therefore, God is not a King, and God is not a Lord, and we cannot confuse metaphors for the real thing. Think of the damage done to women, LGBTQI+ people, and the environment because so many Christians think of God as a literal father and embrace maleness as an actual characteristic of God. Recognizing the limitations of traditional metaphors and constructing new metaphors are key task for ecofeminist theologians as they move toward theologies that support the flourishing of the Earth and its inhabitants.

Metaphorical language is not static but is a process. Metaphors operate like a story, moving from here to there, from "what is" to "what might be" (TeSelle 1975, 33), providing deeper meaning and depth to concepts that are difficult to comprehend. Metaphors help us access realities that may otherwise be inaccessible through literal language. For ecofeminist theologians, metaphors are a powerful way to express connections between the Divine and the natural world and to affirm the goodness of the material world.

BODY, SPIRIT, AND GOD

Christianity emerged under Greco-Roman philosophy, which promoted and emphasized dualism. Dualism divides the world into a dichotomy, and in such a worldview, the spirit is good, and the body is evil; heaven is good, Earth is bad; men are good, and women are bad. The body within Christianity has been viewed negatively as the spirit is preferred over the body. We see, however, that God actually embraces materiality in the prologue to John's gospel, which affirms that the word is made flesh in incarnation. Feminist theologians do not limit incarnation only to Jesus, but rather contend that God is present in all the universe. When Moses asks God, "Show me your glory," we can see God in the world around us. McFague says we recognize the extraordinariness of the ordinary and beauty in creation as a sacrament of the living God because all of creation contains the breath of the living God. We are only alive because the living God is in us (2013, 61, 62). Dualism, which has persisted into contemporary Christianity, maintains a dichotomy and separation between body and spirit, but feminist theologians argue these are not separate entities. Rather, God is present in the world in the flesh because God is in each and every particle of the universe.

The Spirit is the breath, or life-giving power, of the living God. Spirit of God is all around us giving us life. According to ecofeminist theologians, we live within the body of God and this knowledge should motivate us to save the body of God which is being destroyed by our careless and selfish actions. We are all within God, and God is within us. The harm caused to our environment, to God, and ourselves is a cry for justice. To help us understand this intimate connection between God and creation, ecofeminist theologians have proposed the metaphor of the Earth as God's body as a way to challenge the dualism that has perpetuated environmental degradation and subordination of women and other minoritized people.

THE EARTH AS GOD'S BODY

Sallie McFague proposed the metaphor of the Earth as God's body as a way to encourage ecofeminist reflection on the ways humans treat the environment. Suggesting the Earth as God's body is not pantheistic (everything is God) but panentheistic (God is in everything). As Ernest M. Conradie and Willie James Jennings note, ecofeminist theologians appreciate "what is immanent, material, bodily, and earthly, polemically directed against a (male?) emphasis on what is transcendent, ideal, spiritual, and heavenly. Such feminist creation theologies are therefore drawn toward forms of panentheism in order to overcome the dual challenges of deism (God's utter transcendence) and pantheism (God's complete immanence)" (2025, 11).

Even traditional Christianity believes that divine reality is mediated through the material world, a belief traditionally expressed in the Chalcedonian formula that Christ was "fully God, fully man." Ecofeminist theologies radicalize and expand this mediation to include the entire cosmos. As the Word is made flesh, God is with us only through the mediation of embodiment. Like Moses, we are offered not God's face, but God's back—a body that is given (McFague 2013, 64). While God is more than bodies, more than materiality, all bodies, including inanimate bodies, are reflections of God.

The metaphor of the Earth as God's body puts focus on the physical, the lowly, the mundane, the specific, the vulnerable, the invisible, and the other. Bodies with all their differences share characteristics within the body of God. The incarnation of God shows us that we don't see God face to face, but only through the mediation of the bodies that are around us (McFague 2013, 64, 65). We come to know and see God present in broken bodies, abused bodies, invisible bodies, and assaulted bodies around us. God is present within all these various bodies, and, through some of this brokenness, we still find some hope that God's presence in these bodies will bring healing, energy, light, and life. This metaphor of the Earth as God's body is a metaphor that challenges us to do good in the world, as God is present in every particle of it. It emboldens us to work for justice to save the planet from destruction and also to love one another, who shows us the body of God. Ecofeminist theologians call us to move away from patriarchal images and metaphors about God, which allow us to dominate the Earth and damage the Earth. Instead, they challenge us to reimagine new and liberative ways and metaphors to speak about the materiality of God, which will move us to work toward saving the Earth.

Tongan Roman Catholic theologian, Sr. Keiti Ann Kanongata'a believes that women's stories are the basis or starting point of doing theology. It is everyday life stories that provide the materials to do theology. The effects of climate change on Tongans' homes have political and theological implications that can be addressed by Tongan women's stories. She compares theology in the Pacific to birthing, as they are both important and symbolic images in Oceania. The Earth is God's body which is giving birth to new life. This image becomes a powerful motivator for those who are working to save the planet. It is an image that involves Tongans' understanding of the land, sea, and motherhood (Kanongata'a,1992, 4). The image of the God giving birth to the Earth calls all people to nurture and take care of the Earth.

ESCHATOLOGY

Eschatology is the study of the end times or the final vision of the Divine plan within Christian theology. Ecofeminist theology is especially concerned with eschatology because of the dire future climate change presages and the climate disaster's disruption to the Divine plan for health, wholeness, and peace for all the universe. For ecofeminists, eschatology offers an ethical challenge to our present overconsumption, pollution, and apathy toward nature.

Biblical eschatological reflections include justice for all of God's creation. The waters in the book of Revelation cry out for justice, and the martyrs cry out, "How Long, O Lord?" In trying to develop an eschatology of healing that can help us in a time of climate injustice, we need to expand our images of justice and judgment so that the scenes of judgment can address structural sin (Rossing 2017, 332). Structural sin, the embeddedness of racism, sexism, and other forms of intersecting oppressions in social institutions, fosters environmental degradation through corporate greed, political power, inadequate education, limited research into environmental polluters, lack of access to healthcare, war, and religious justification for dominance and control. The Korean term *han* reminds us to fight back against structural sin and systemic injustices that get embedded into our society, culture, and religion. We need to recognize them and eliminate them so that we can eliminate *han*.

On the global scene, the Western world must accept responsibility for becoming the source of *han* for the global South and developing countries. Due to Western greed and colonialism, the West takes more than its fair share of resources and, in the process, destroys the Earth. Western corporations commercialize natural resources, export them around the world, and sell them at exorbitant profits, stripping natural resources from poorer nations, decreasing biodiversity, and even leading some species to extinction. This environmental degradation widens social and economic gaps between the rich and the poor, creating even greater vulnerabilities for the poorest people in the world, most of whom are women and children.

Ecofeminist theologians call for people with greater resources to rethink their consumption and refuse to contribute to the exploitation of the environment and other people by multinational corporations. Ecofeminists encourage people to embrace simpler, more sustainable lifestyles that consume fewer resources. This shift is essential to eliminate *han*—a deep cultural expression of suffering and oppression—and to move toward a life marked by "enoughness," where balance, justice, and mutual care define our relationship with the Earth and one another. Ecofeminist theology looks at how *han* is not just personal but cosmic as it reflects the broken relationships between humanity, creation, and the divine. Therefore, "enoughness" is not about scarcity but about balance, gratitude, and the right relationships—with ourselves, with others, with the Earth, and with God. It's a call to live justly, compassionately, and consciously in a world aching for healing.

More central in the book of Revelation than the final judgment found in Revelation 20 is the judgment of Babylon found in Revelation 17–18. This passage describes the fall of the Roman Empire, imaged through an anticipatory funeral for the unjust economy. The passage has a three-fold lament for the rulers, the merchants, and the mariners (Rev 18:9-20), showing a model we can emulate today. It draws the imagery of a funeral in advance from Isaiah 14, performatively enacting the end of the Roman economic system via satirical dirge songs, "Alas, alas, alas" (Rev 18:10, 16, 19). Revelation's funeral liturgy for Babylon/Rome is a funeral we also can perform to announce the "end of the system of this world" today, the fossil fuel economy that devours lands and peoples (Rossing 2017, 332). The eschatology found in the Bible reminds us of what we need to do to save ourselves. We need to turn away from destructive ways of living so the *han* we are causing to nature, creation, and the world will be released, and the Earth can heal and flourish.

RELEASING *HAN* AND SAVING THE PLANET

Climate change is drastically causing harm, suffering, and pain to the Earth. We need to alleviate the Earth's suffering and *han*. Ecofeminist theologians lead the way in rethinking God and God's presence in the world in relation to nature. They argue that through the power and actions of God, *han* and the negative effects of *han* can be overcome. Ecofeminist theologians see one goal of a Christian life to be "wholeness" as well as "holiness." To achieve wholeness, all of nature needs to heal from injustice, abuse, and violence. This wholeness can be achieved by addressing *han* and eliminating it.

In this globalized world, ecofeminist theologians argue, it is crucial to recognize that we need a new worldview, one which will reform the systems that have produced *han* in the world. We need to think of our world in terms of interconnectedness. We need to recognize that all of us are dependent on one another, that we do not understand who we are until we understand our interrelatedness with others. When we realize that others' *han* is our *han*, and vice versa, we enter into a new dimension of true human nature. We know little of our *han* unless we know the *han* of others. If we realize our indivisible interconnectedness everyone, including oppressors, can cooperate to dissolve the *han* of the oppressed.

Within this recognition of globalization and consumerism, we need to work toward downscaling. People in the developed world need to live with less and consume less so that the world can survive. We need to develop and promote "enoughness" and make sacrifices so that others might live. We need to acknowledge that we have more than we need, and we need to be able to share our abundance with others. If all consume less, then the planet can support more; if some consume more, then others must consume less.

An ecofeminist eschatology contends that the final aim of creation is not judgement and destruction but wholeness, justice, and peace for all the universe. The world is not moving toward some divinely determined apocalypse; in fact, the apocalypse we may face because of climate change is the antithesis of Divine desire. Rather, God's aim is for creation is for each entity to achieve wholeness, to be creative and novel, and to express God's love in relation to all other entities.

There are different ways of viewing the world that will help us toward saving the planet. One is to see the Earth as a corporation with a collection of individual human beings drawn together to benefit its members by optimal use of natural resources. The second is to see the planet more like an organism that survives and prospers through the interrelationship and interdependence of its many parts, both human and non-human. The first model seems "natural" to most middle-class Westerners, while the second model seems utopian. The first model is injurious to nature and to poor people, while the other one would be healthier for the planet and all its inhabitants (McFague 2001, 72, 73). In this light, we need to value models of viewing the Earth with the hopes of saving the planet. We have caused too much damage to the Earth. But if we can view the Earth more like an organism in which each part affects the others, then we can try to reverse some of the damage that has already been done to the Earth.

We need to work toward the well-being of the planet and justice for all people. We can work toward releasing our *han* and the *han* of others and the Earth as we strive to live a simpler life. As we begin to live out this new life, we can work toward the elimination of unjust suffering. The elimination of *han* from one's life and others is a liberating and powerful experience that will change us and the world.

EARTH AS GOD'S HOUSEHOLD

Sallie McFague offers the metaphor of the world as God's household or *oikos* (2001, 36). McFague suggests we see our planet as a house that we can care for rather than a place of endless resources from which we take for our personal use and gratification. The word "ecology" comes from the Greek *oikos* (house/home) so ecology is essentially the study of organisms in their home (McFague 1993, 56). If we can focus our attention on the Earth as a home, we may become better caretakers of our planet for future generations to come. Joyce Ann Mercer adds, "Christian theology needs to put forward a similarly critical, active, constructive vision of hope—an eschatology that links how humans inhabit God's *oikos* in the present with bold, imaginative visions of what life as creatures among others embedded in a common home might look like for all to flourish" (Mercer 2022, 10).

Our daily living habits contribute to the planet's deterioration as we continuously pollute and damage the Earth. We must change our ways immediately before we do greater irreversible harm to the Earth. The Greek word, *metanoia*, means to repent and change direction. Ecofeminist theologians call us to repent from our overconsumption, degradation of the environment, and harm to the planet and its inhabitants, particularly the most vulnerable and marginalized. Environmental pollution and climate change have the greatest impact on people who are poor and made vulnerable by their poverty. The rich do the most damage to the environment. The poor become displaced, lose homes, lose jobs, and lose a healthy way of living due to the greed of rich nations and individuals. Jesus told his followers to feed the hungry and clothe the naked. Ecofeminist theologians say we must do likewise for our neighbors and victims of climate change. We must also rethink the Christian faith and center it not only on humanity but also on all of God's creation. This challenges us to refocus on God in order to change our ways to reimagine a new way of living that promotes sustainability, love, and solidarity. Without a healthy planet, humans cannot survive. Therefore, as humans live amid self-destruction, they need to come before God and work together for change. Viewing the planet as God's household can challenge us to take care of our home and to see all beings and all nature itself as our relations to whom we owe care. If we attend to the household, we can move toward sustainability, justice, peace, and flourishing.

BIBLIOGRAPHY

Bauman, Whitney A. 2018. "Queer Values for a Queer Climate: Developing a Versatile Planetary Ethic," In *Meaningful Flesh: Reflections on Religion and Nature for a Queer Planet*, Eds. W. A. Bauman & W. A. Goleta. Punctum Books.

Carroll, Seforosa. 2022. "Climate Change, Faith and Theology in the Pacific (Oceania): the Role of Faith Inbuilding Resilient Communities." *Practical Theology*, 15 (5): 409–419.

Conradie, Ernst M. and Willie James Jennings. 2025. "The Place of Creation in Christian Ecotheology—Some Shifts in the Story," p. 1–24. In *The Place of Story and the Story of Place: An Earthed Faith: Telling the Story Amid the Anthropocene*, Eds. Ernst M. Conradie & Willie James Jennings. Pickwick Publications.

Erickson, Jacob J. 2018. "Irreverent Theology: On the Queer Ecology of Creation," In *Meaningful Flesh: Reflections on Religion and Nature for a Queer Planet*, Eds. W. A. Bauman & W. A. Goleta. Punctum Books.

Gebara, Ivone. 2017. "Women's Suffering, Climate Injustice, God, and Pope Francis's Theology: Some Insights from Brazil," p. 67–80. In *Planetary Solidarity*, Eds. Grace Ji-Sun Kim & Hilda Koster. Fortress Press.

Harris, Melanie L. 2016. "Ecowomanism: An Introduction." *Worldviews*, 20 (1): 5–14.

Johnson, Elizabeth A. 2024. *Come, Have Breakfast: Meditations on God and the Earth*. Orbis Books.

Kanongata'a, Keiti Ann. 1992. "A Pacific Women's Theology of Birthing and Liberation." *Pacific Journal of Theology Series*, 7: 3–11.

McFague, Sallie. 1993. *The Body of God: An Ecological Theology*. Fortress Press.

McFague, Sallie. 2001. *Life Abundant*. Fortress Press.

McFague, Sallie. 2013. "A Meditation on Exodus 23:33b," p. 61. In *Sallie McFague: Collected Readings*, Ed. David B. Lott.. Fortress Press.

Mercer, Joyce Ann. 2022. "Children and Climate Anxiety: An Ecofeminist Practical Theological Perspective." *Religions*, 13: 302. https://doi.org/10.3390/rel13040302. Accessed April 6, 2025.

Nortjé-Meyer, Lily. 2022. "The Intersection of Flesh (σὰρξ): An Eco-Feminist Incentive for Animals, Women, and the Logos as Interconnected Flesh," p. 129–155. In *Feminist Interpretations of Biblical Literature*, Ed. Nortjé-Meyer. Lily. Cambridge Scholars.

Park, Andrew Sung. 1993. *The Wounded Heart of God*. Abingdon Press.

Rossing, Barbara R. 2017. Reimagining Eschatology: Toward Healing and Hope for a World at the Eschatos," p. 325–348. In *Planetary Solidarity*, Eds. Grace Ji-Sun Kim & Hilda Koster. Fortress Press.

Spencer, Daniel T. 2018. "Religion, Nature, and Queer Theory," In *Meaningful Flesh: Reflections on Religion and Nature for a Queer Planet*, Eds. W. A. Bauman & W. A. Goleta. Punctum Books.

TeSelle, Sallie. 1975. *Speaking in Parables: A Study in Metaphor and Theology*. Fortress Press.

POSTCOLONIAL FEMINIST THEOLOGIES

Colonialism is the conquest and control of other people's land and goods. It has been a recurrent and widespread feature of human history (Loomba 2005, 8). Since the 16th century, dominant forms of colonialism have been the expansion of various European powers into Asia, Africa, or the Americas. The consequences of colonialism have been grave, dangerous, and even deadly as colonizers went into different parts of the world to conquer in the name of Christianity or in the name of "civilization" as European colonizers viewed the inhabitants of other lands as backward, barbaric, and unintelligent. Colonialism did not end with the conquest of the Americas, Africa, and Asia. It continues in different forms. For example, today, we see the United States spreading its empire around the world by building military bases in other countries, taking American ideologies and cultural practices to other communities through aid and economic globalization, and, most recently, threatening the conquest of Canada and Greenland. Even within the United States itself, the colonization of Indigenous people continues, with some of the right recently declaring that Indigenous people are not birthright citizens of the United States. Not surprisingly, colonialism also intersects with sexism, misogyny, homophobia, and transphobia, and colonial powers further subjugate women, children, and LGBTQI+Q people through violence, exploitation, and invisibility.

In such a context and time, postcolonial feminist theology has become an important lens, tool, and method of doing theology to understand how to engage in liberative theologies, which can empower the colonized and challenge the colonizers. Postcolonialism is the study of the social, political, and economic impacts of colonialism and the ongoing consequences of its subjugation of entire nations, continents, and peoples. Using a postcolonial lens allows us to examine the historic and ongoing harms of colonialism, while a postcolonial feminist lens ensures we examine how gender and other intersecting categories of difference operate within colonial and postcolonial frameworks and experiences. Postcolonial feminist theology turns a postcolonial feminist eye onto the role of theology in perpetuating colonial domination of women and other minoritized people and counters traditional colonizing theologies (those that justify colonization) with liberatory theologies that empower social transformation, equity, and justice.

Postcolonial feminist theology asks critical questions about colonialism, race, and gender in relation to God. Postcolonial feminist theologians understand that gender difference and inequality cannot be analyzed by a false universal (white) feminist theology and therefore they takes seriously the religious practices of women living under colonialism (Higgs 2017, 79). There is never one postcolonial feminist theology for everyone as women's contexts and experiences differ across cultures and nations. Postcolonial feminist theology is a contextual theology that takes seriously the experiences of colonialism in the ways women and other minoritized people think about God.

COLONIALISM

European colonialism involved techniques and patterns of domination that penetrated societies to help grow European capitalism and industry. Indian literary scholar Ania Loomba believes that modern colonialism did more than extract goods and wealth from the countries the colonizers conquered; it restructured economies to create complex relationships between colonizers and colonized to ensure a smooth flow of human and natural resources between colonized and colonial countries (Loomba 2005, 9, 10). Colonizers profited at the expense of the colonized. They depleted colonized people's natural resources, as well as their economic, religious, and cultural status. Colonized people became an extension of the colonized and existed for the colonizers. Christianity has often been a tool of colonizers, justifying the missionary enterprise that serves the economic interests of colonial powers and validating the subordination of women.

Colonialism has done immense damage as it has systematically subjugated and oppressed the colonized. Women have been doubly colonized, subjugated both as colonized people and women. They are treated as sexual objects who can be violated at the whim of the colonizer. Colonialism has often involved enslavement, and colonizers have taken girls and women as sexual slaves. Today, we see women used in global networks of sex trafficking and sexual enslavement. The mistreatment and deaths of so many women under colonialism motivate postcolonial feminist theologians to cry out for justice. As postcolonial feminist theologian Kwok Pui-lan notes, if Christianity has played such a significant role in colonial conquest, theology must be involved in postcolonial strategies to overcome empire (2021, 11). Postcolonial feminist theology is desperately needed to challenge past and present colonization of women and other minority people and to help oppressed peoples in their struggles for liberation from imperial power. In particular, it is essential to decolonize Christian theology itself and end Christianity's complicity with colonial projects.

POSTCOLONIAL THEORY

The word postcolonial has been coined to describe the modern history of imperialism, struggles for independence, and neocolonialist realities. This definition emphasizes the connection and continuity between the past and the present, between the colonizer and the colonized, and the devastating impact colonialism continues to have on the exploited people. Postcolonial theory studies the cultural, political, and economic consequences of colonialism and imperialism and their long-lasting effects on the colonized. In this context, colonialism centers the experiences of those living under colonial power, while imperialism centers the subjugating power of the empire.

Batswana postcolonial feminist biblical critic Musa W. Dube believes that while postcolonial theory recognizes the importance of analyzing the colonial past, its greater concern is the continuing negative consequences of colonialism and the possibilities for liberation, transformation, and freedom (Dube 2000, 15). The ongoing damage of colonialism continues to ruin people's lives, cultures, and societies, and, thus, postcolonial theory works to subvert empire and the damage it continues to do to people, their land, and their resources.

As with other theories of liberation, many postcolonial theories have often assumed men's experiences and perspectives and omitted analysis of gender, race, sexuality, and other intersecting categories of identity. Postcolonial feminist theory fills in this gap by moving women and other minoritized people to the center of analysis, recognizing a plurality of oppressions, and acknowledging multiple identities based on class, education, sexuality, race, ethnicity, and gender (Sugirtharajah 2001, 262). Within the empire, these intersecting categories of identity work to oppress minoritized people, not only through the taking of land and resources but also through the colonizing of minds so that colonized people accept their subjugation and go along with the desires of the colonizers. Postcolonial feminist theory analyzes the ways different forms of oppression work together to continue to oppress colonized women and other minoritized groups by shaping the experiences of colonialism in specific ways around gender, race, and other categories. This analysis is foundational for postcolonial feminist theologies, which apply postcolonial feminist lenses to questions of faith.

POSTCOLONIAL READING OF SCRIPTURE

Many people who read the Bible rarely think about it in its colonial context, but the Bible was written by authors who lived as colonizers and colonized. Even the history of the uses of the Bible itself carries a long history of readings to justify the taking of other people's lands and resources and to empower struggle against forces of colonization. A careful and liberative reading of the Bible demands postcolonial interpretations of the Bible to understand the colonialism of the past and present and to inspire movement toward a future with the liberation of the colonized. Postcolonial biblical criticism engages in constructive theological discourse as it rereads biblical texts with postcolonial concerns at the center. It is sensitive to subaltern and feminine elements embedded in the texts. It interacts with and reflects on postcolonial circumstances such as hybridity, fragmentation, deterritorialization, and hyphenated, double, or multiple identities. The religious landscape is complex, and to read a text through one single religious view is not helpful (Sugirtharajah 2001, 252). Therefore, we need to listen to the diverse voices of the colonized to interpret scripture and to help make sense in our postcolonial context today.

Postcolonial readings also require a humility that recognizes the limitations of any one interpreter's standpoint. While individual interpreters may have their own theological, confessional, and denominational stance, this should not exclude them from exploring a variety of religious truth claims. Because no one person or denomination, for that matter, can know all truths, postmodern biblical criticism encourages readers of the Bible to make room for different, and even competing, interpretations that offer insights into diverse experiences. Postcolonial theology believes that liberation and its praxis must come from the collective unconscious of the people. It sees liberation not as something hidden in the text but rather as a process born of public consensus created in a dialogue between text and context. In other words, liberation comes not in the biblical text but from the interplay between people, communities, cultures, and texts. The Bible, then, is not the adjudicator of morality or ethics but is rather one among many factors that are part of the struggle for liberation. This is a different approach from other biblical hermeneutics, which believe there is always something liberative within the biblical texts. This approach challenges our liberation theological hermeneutics that seeks liberation within the biblical text and asks us to be open to different theological truths outside the Bible.

Postcolonial feminist biblical scholar, Musa Dube, tries to "cultivate postcolonial strategies of reading the Bible that resist and decolonize both patriarchy and imperial oppression" (Dube 2000, 43). She reads the Bible culturally and with a desire to resist empire as imperialism is woven into Christianity and Judaism. We see throughout the Bible that, at times, the people of Israel live in subjugation to colonial powers; at other times, they are the colonial powers invading other people's lands and claiming them as their own. Christianity began under the colonial power of the Roman Empire and soon extended its own colonial power as it became complicit with political rulers and governments. We see these attitudes toward empire throughout the Bible. Some passages in the First Testament warn Israelites against marrying foreign women because they are not pure. Other passages extoll the virtue of welcoming the foreigner. Some passages encourage conquering and pillaging other nations; other passage imagine nations at peace with one another.

As noted in Chapter 2, one First Testament story demonstrates clearly the complexities of colonization. In Joshua 2 and 6, we meet Rahab, who lives in Jericho in Canaan. Rahab is colonized as a woman by her own people, a prostitute who lives on the margins of the city. When Joshua sends spies to scope out the city for conquest, they meet Rahab, who conspires with them on the condition they save her and her family when they conquer the city. The conquerors spare Rahab, and she lives the rest of her life in Israel. Rahab is "doubly colonized," by the Canaanite patriarchy and by the imperial force of the Israelite patriarchy. As a doubly colonized woman, she is used by both sides and yet, in the midst of her limited options, she finds a way to survive and save her family. To understand the complexities of Rahab as a doubly colonized woman, we need a multi-lens postcolonial hermeneutical approach that helps produce a liberating biblical reading for colonized women (Higgs 2017, 85).

Postcolonial criticism takes the "other," who are namely the poor, seriously. Postcolonial feminist criticism recognizes that the poor are disproportionately women and other minoritized people, and it asks why that is true. Postcolonial feminist biblical critics seek to dismantle hegemonic interpretations to allow the voices of the other to be heard and valued. Postcolonial readings see the Bible and biblical interpretation as a site of struggle over efficacy, meanings, and power. Postcolonialism is guarded in its approach to the Bible as it sees the Bible as both a safe and an unsafe text. Too often, the Bible has provided justification for colonialism, and many interpreters have used the Bible to forgive the church its entanglements in colonial atrocities (Sugirtharajah 2001, 259). Dominant interpretations of the Bible supported colonialism and its atrocities, and this history of interpretation reminds us that the Bible needs to be read with caution and with awareness of cultural contexts in order for it to be of use in liberatory struggles. For colonized women, this approach also demands attention to gender, recognizing that colonization is a gendered process with differential impacts on women and LGBTQI+Q people. Even within colonized cultures, many Christians may read the Bible to subjugate women as the subordinate other within the other.

HYBRIDITY AND THEOLOGY

The word "hybrid" is developed from biological and botanical origins and in Latin it means the offspring of a tame sow and a wild boar. A hybrid can be defined as a mongrel or mule, an animal or plant, produced from the mixture of two species. Hybridization is a mixture of two things. Hybridity brings together, and fuses, but also maintains separation (Young 1995, 6, 22). This mixing of two things occurs in all aspects of our life as things are not homogenous but are rather heterogeneous.

Postcoloniality is about acquiring a new identity. During colonialism, there is an intermingling of people and cultures, and the result is a hybridized identity (Sugirtharajah 1998, 6). Hybridity is a pragmatic exercise of power and agency, reflecting a very grassroots and contextualized approach to cultural, economic, and political survival in contexts of pervasive structural evil (Jones & Lakeland 2005, 156). *Mestiza* is an example of hybridity. The hybrid mestiza body provides a model of human interrelationality, as it is "inscribed by the multiple relations from which it emerges" (Rivera 2007, 96). The mixing of people occurs as well as cultural and religious hybridity. Hybridity becomes a resistance to colonial power. Grace Ji-Sun Kim emphasizes, "The postcolonial concept of hybridity is an especially helpful way to analyze the characteristics and experience of oppression in the context of colonization, so that these people can lay claim to their own agency" (2020, 601).

Hybridity is a form of resistance as it dispenses with dualistic and hierarchical constructions of cultures, which are used to claim the superiority of colonizing cultures. Hybridity shows that cultures grow and are dependent on borrowing from each other (Dube 2000, 51). A culture is never stable but is ongoing changes, modifications, and mixings. Hybridity works organically, hegemonizing, creating new spaces, structures, and scenes, and intentionally diasporizing, intervening as a form of subversion, translation, and transformation (Young 1995, 25). Hybridity creates new spaces from which one can recognize one's position. It also creates this space to articulate one's experiences, struggles, and joys. It offers a space to bring about a transformation that can alter how one does theology and brings praxis into our theology.

Hybridity becomes a potent lens to explore interculturation in the postcolonial world (Ramazani 2001, 6). Society is not monolithic nor homogenous but rather is mixed, and this mingling of cultures creates interculturalism. There is not one culture, but always many cultures that co-exist together. As multiple cultures interrelate, differences intersect to create new cultures and ways of being.

While some have termed the mingling of societies as multiculturalism, the term suggests the multiple cultures simply exist together, side by side. But the reality is that when cultures come together, they collide, mix, integrate, synthesize, and acculturate themselves. In this way, postcolonial society is not merely a multicultural society but a hybrid society. In hybridity, a new product emerges. It is not just a mosaic of cultures existing next to each other, but it is an intermingling of societies. Each culture mixes with other cultures to produce different distinct cultures which are different from the original. In hybridity, something changes within the inner core of society.

Hybridity challenges and revalues the fixed assumptions of colonial identity by exposing the instability of dominant narratives. It emerges through the repetition and disruption of discriminatory identity constructs, revealing the cracks in colonial power. The colonial hybrid occupies an ambivalent space—a space where power is both asserted and unsettled, and where desire and resistance intersect. In this in-between space, the dominant discourse begins to fracture, splitting along the axis of its claim to be both representative and authoritative. Hybridity thus becomes a powerful tool for undermining colonial control, opening up new possibilities for identity, agency, and meaning (Bhabha 1994, 112, 113). Hybridity is about ambivalence, and this is something to be welcomed and not dismissed. Not everything is clear and straightforward but can be ambiguous and ambivalent.

Indian-born literary and cultural theorist, Leela Gandhi states that hybridity helps destabilize colonized cultures (Gandhi 1998, 136). Hybridity embraces both anti-colonial and anti-essentialist strategies in confronting and challenging established hegemonies. It is common for marginalized people to be perceived as "others" and develop a "double consciousness" (the ability to see from both their own and the oppressors' perspectives) in the process of cultural hybridization (Li 2002, 130). This hybrid double consciousness should be embraced as it provides new ways of thinking and being and offers insights into experiences of and struggles against colonialism. It is especially useful to minoritized people as it provides a way to account for their intersectional experiences of oppression across colonialism, sexism, racism, heterosexism, and other systems of oppression. The formation of hyphenated, fractured, multiple, and multiplying identities acts as a challenge to the binary logic of colonialism and the assumption of fixed identities that is a tenet of colonial oppression.

Attempts to embrace hybridized identities are often dismissed under the label of syncretism. These critiques are rooted in Western Christian frameworks of exclusivity, superiority, and expansionism, which prioritize doctrinal purity and hierarchical authority over lived experience and contextual wisdom. However, hybridity is a complex and dynamic process of cultural negotiation and transformation. It reflects a deeper engagement with multiple identities, traditions, and histories. Hybridity does not simply reject provincial, national, or imperial attachments—it works through them, reshaping them in the pursuit of a more inclusive and liberating vision (Sugirtharajah 1998, 16). In this way, hybridity becomes a site of creative resistance and spiritual reclamation, offering new ways of being and believing that transcend binary thinking and rigid borders. Hybridity becomes a sacred tool of survival and renewal. It makes room for voices at the margins to reinterpret sacred texts and reshape theological discourse that honors and celebrates human diversity. Therefore, hybridity is not a threat to theology but a necessity.

Hybridity shifts the conceptualization of identity as not a stable point but of liminality, instability, impurity, movement, and fluidity. The postcolonial notion of hybridity is not the dissolution of differences but the renegotiation of structures of power built on differences. It is not synonymous with assimilation, as assimilation is something that the colonialists and later the nativists advocated as a way to integrate diverse people into the values and practices of dominant hierarchies without changing the dominant culture. Rather, hybridity is a two-way process where both parties are interactive, so something new is created and produced. Given the multiple contexts in which Christianity is practiced, hybridity calls for the reform of Christian identity within the postcolonial context (Sugirtharajah 1998, 125, 126). Hybridity is a powerful tool to examine and understand the self and context.

Hybridization involves fusion, the creation of a new form, which can then be set against the old form, of which it is partly made up. Hybridity makes one from multiple distinct things and cleaves distinct things into multiples, turning difference into sameness and sameness into difference, but in a way that makes the same no longer the same, the different no longer simply different (Young 1995, 25, 26). A new creation comes forth as hybridity mixes and gives birth to new beings.

Postcolonial thinkers must confront oppressive aspects in their own indigenous systems of gender and reinterpret the old, promote the good, and imagine the new in the hybrid spaces of the native culture (Dube 2002, 116). As this happens, new ways of being will emerge which will provide new paths for subjugated women to move out of their subordination.

DECOLONIZING THEOLOGY

In many ways, theology has been a driver of empire, often serving to legitimize systems of colonialism, patriarchy, and domination. Therefore, theology itself must be decolonized—a process that involves contesting, critiquing, and dismantling the imperial frameworks embedded within Christian thought. This involves removing colonial aspects from existing theological constructs and replacing them with liberative alternatives rooted in justice and equity.

Decolonizing theology requires an honest interrogation of Christianity's complicity in empire-building and the maintenance of hegemonic power structures. It also demands the inclusion of intersectional perspectives which center on voices that have been historically silenced, such as those of Indigenous peoples, women of color, people with disabilities, queer people, and others who experience marginalization and oppression (Dube 2002, 19). Through this, new theological narratives, symbols, and categories can emerge that do not reinforce systems of oppression but instead embody solidarity, healing, and liberation. Decolonized theology does not erase faith but renews it by anchoring it in radical love and embodied truth.

Decolonizing theology involves revealing the Eurocentric assumptions that underlie traditional theologies and ways theology is produced by and for white Westerners. Feminist postcolonial theology must analyze gender and race and challenge the center, which is dominated by empire and patriarchy. The

Bible includes heroes and chosen peoples going into lands and conquering them. Christian theology's practice of rationalizing their conquest has been a consistent method to justify colonialism which is something which needs to be diminished. Biblical scholarship that fails to recognize the imperialism of the Bible will only end up reinforcing it and therefore is unable to resist imperialism (Dube 2000, 57) and (neo)colonialism. Decolonizing theology needs to critique the spiritual violence of missionary conquest of land and people. It needs to call out the violence of erasure and advocate for liberation from colonialism.

HYBRID THEOLOGY

Postcolonial theology is not limited to traditional theological or even religious sources. Rather, postcolonial theologies work toward liberation in response to voices within and outside the biblical tradition (Sugirtharajah 2001, 262). Hybridity can be a very helpful category for women, especially poor, queer, and women of color who are seeking liberative theological methods to decolonize theology because of its reach beyond traditional sources within the church. Theology has often been used as a trap to bait and bring women into a faith that is patriarchal and destructive. Much of traditional Christian theology serves to colonize diverse people, especially women who become subordinated or subjugated to men. Hybrid theology offers a challenge to traditional white supremacist, patriarchal theologies by bringing a mix of voices, traditions, and knowledge into dialogue with Christian theology, creating a mix of traditions that both maintain their distinct identities and create something new that can serve the needs of liberation. Unlike syncretism which has often appropriated Indigenous ideas and perpetuated colonial dominance, hybridity calls for an equal and shared participation that fully values diverse traditions.

Hybrid theology challenges theological centrality from dominant Western Christianity that has intentionally and unintentionally reproduced exclusionary tendencies. Hybrid theology emerges from the intersections of multiple traditions, cultures, and experiences as it refuses purity or singular authority. Instead, it reimagines theology through multiplicity and contradictions shaped by diasporic identities and postcolonial realities. Hybrid theology unsettles the dominant colonial theological center to open space for new dialogues as it challenges us to see that sacred knowledge is not confined to institutional doctrine but is dispersed and detached.

Postcolonial feminist theologies embrace hybridity as an essential source of theological insight. "Hybridity becomes a form of resistance, for it dispenses with dualistic and hierarchical constructions of cultures" (Dube 2000, 51). Hybrid theology embraces the indigenous religions of hyphenated peoples and intermingles them with Christianity. Hybrid theology draws from the colonized as well as the colonizer to construct theologies useful in liberation. Christianity and indigenous religions are thus not seen as competing opposites but as mutual traditions that enrich each other. Hybridity becomes a decolonizing strategy (Dube 2002, 117) by pointing out the struggles of colonized people around the world, and drawing from various traditions to offer liberating images, theologies, and strategies.

As a postcolonial feminist strategy, hybrid theology seeks to embrace healing, liberation, and empowerment for colonized people, especially women and LGBTQI+ people, and structural transformation to end colonization and create equitable and just institutions and structures. As Hong Kong born postcolonial feminist theologian Kwok Pui-lan explains, core Christian concepts, such as that of the Christ, have no original or privileged status "that can be claimed as pure and foundations, not subject to the limitations of culture and history." She challenges the notion that there is a "Christian essence to be transplanted, transposed, or indigenized in a foreign culture or context." Hybridity, instead, "allows marginalized communities to claim the authority" to advance their own theological claims (2005, 182). She points to the development of the understanding of the Black Christ within Black theology. Black men, she explains, reappropriated blackness in the Christ as a way to oppose white culture and dominance. As, however, blackness neared becoming essentialized in Black liberation thinking, womanist theologians challenged the gender assumptions of the Black Christ to propose more nuanced and fluid meanings (2005, 183). She also draws attention to Asian Christian women to demonstrate the importance of hybridity. She explains that clear differentiation between Christian and Asian traditions has often worked to support colonial power. In response, Asian Christian women have proposed more hybridized theological concepts that take place both across and within cultures.

POSTCOLONIAL FEMINIST THEOLOGY

The goal of postcolonialism is to abolish distinctions between center and periphery as well as all other "binarisms" that are allegedly a legacy of the colonist way of thinking (Dirlik 1994, 329). Postcolonial feminist theology aims to identify, critique, and supplant Christianity's colonizing history and tendencies to ensure a way toward liberation for women and other minoritized people. Postcolonial feminist theology needs to interrogate and analyze the gendered colonizing values, strategies, and effects of mainstream theologies that maintain the imperialistic paradigm of the West (Dube 2000, 19). Imperialism is embedded within theological concepts, methods, and institutions, and thus postcolonial feminist theology must be critical of churches, academic institutions, and theologians for their complicity in the maintenance intersecting systems of colonialism, patriarchy, racism, and classism.

Postcolonial feminist theologies have offered a number of critiques of traditional theologies. They contend traditional theologies have:

- been identified primarily with the West;
- supported Christianity's universal and exclusive claims;
- supported expansion and colonialism in the name of God;
- ignored or downplayed the imperial settings of Christian origins;
- ignored the impact of empire on ancient and modern texts;

- ignored the perspectives of multiply marginalized people;
- ignored ways power is deployed in biblical texts;
- ignored ways gender inequality maintains structures of colonialism and imperial power;
- ignored or reinforced antisemitic biases in Christian thought;
- created discourses of Otherness and inferiority applied to entire peoples and continents;
- failed to critique the imperialism of the missionary movement; and
- been done through a cis-, white, heteropatriarchal lens.

To counter these shortcomings of traditional theologies, postcolonial feminist theologies seek to construct theologies and practices which challenge dominant Western interpretations and their colonizing effects, particularly on women. Postcolonial feminist theologies, therefore, begin with an interrogation of traditional and other feminist theologies for their colonial entanglements. Postcolonial feminist theologies recognize that feminist theologies are not immune to colonialism. Too often theologies constructed by predominantly white Western feminist theologians overlook the effects of colonialism on or even the justification of ongoing colonization and may serve as colonizing forces themselves. Postcolonial feminist theologians, instead, work to reconstruct theologies from perspectives of postcolonial concerns. In additional to traditional sources of theology, they also use of storytelling, social analysis, poetry, art, symbols, and rituals as ways to draw on diverse ways of knowing. They are intersectional at their core, recognizing the diversity of women's experiences in relation to race/ethnicity, nation, social class, sexuality, age, ability, and religion. in connection with their shared experience of colonialism. That means, for example, postcolonial feminist theologians avoid oversimplifying identities or working from a single-axis perspective (focused only on gender or only on ethnicity, for example).

Kwok Pui-lan offers the image of a "diasporic imagination" as a key method for postcolonial feminist theology. She says diasporic imagination is like a storyteller who "selects pieces, fragments, and legends from her cultural and historical memory to weave together tales that are passed from generation to generation. These talks are refashioned and retold in each generation, with new material added, to face new circumstances and to reinvent the identity of a people. She continues, offering a "female diasporic subject as multiply located, always doubly displaced, and having to negotiate an ambivalent past, while holding on to the fragments of memories, cultures, and histories in order to dream of a different future" (2005, 46)

Kwok explains that the task of postcolonial feminist theology revolves around three loci, which are closely related to one another: resignifying gender, requeering sexuality, and redoing theology (2005, 128). Kwok calls for a reexamination of the ways (predominantly) white feminists have thought about gender so that it becomes intersectional. She notes, in particular, how white feminists often fail to critique colonialism or assume a white subject. Similarly, she points out the inherent heteronormativity of most theology and calls for a centering of queer sexuality, recognizing the potential of queer sexuality to" subvert colonial desire" (2005, 142). Finally, she says, postcolonial feminist theology must reconceptualize the relationship between theology and empire through intersectional lenses. She challenges feminist theology not simply to adapt traditional Christian theological themes in a reformist approach but rather to begin in a feminist analysis of the postcolonial condition and articulate theological themes from there.

BIBLIOGRAPHY

Bhabha, Homi K. 1994. *The Location of Culture*. Routledge.

Dirlik, Arif. 1994. "Postcolonial Aura: Third World Criticism in the Age of Global Capitalism." *Critical Inquiry*, 20: 328–356.

Dube, Musa W. 2000. *Postcolonial Feminist Interpretation of the Bible*. St. Chalice Press.

Dube, Musa W. 2002. "Postcoloniality, Feminist Spaces, and Religion," p. 100–120. In *Postcolonialism, Feminism and Religious Discourse*, Eds. Laura E. Donaldson & Kwok Pui-lan. Routledge.

Gandhi, Leela. 1998. *Postcolonial Theory: A Critical Introduction*. Columbia University Press.

Higgs, Eleanor Tiplady. 2017. "Postcolonial Feminist Theologies," p. 79–83. In *Gender: God*, Ed. M. Sian. Macmillan.

Jones, Serene and Paul Lakeland, Eds. 2005. *Constructive Theology: A Contemporary Approach to Classical Themes*. Fortress Press.

Kim, Grace Ji-Sun. 2020. "Postcolonial Theology and Intersectionality." *Journal of Ecumenical Studies*. 55 (4): 595–608.

Kwok, Pui-lan. 2005. *Postcolonial Imagination and Feminist Theology*. Westminster John Knox.

Kwok, Pui-lan. 2021. *Postcolonial Politics and Theology: Unraveling Empire for a Global World*. Westminster John Knox.

Li, Huey-li. 2002. "From Alterity to Hybridity: A Query of Double Consciousness." *Philosophy of Education*. 138–146.

Loomba, Ania. 2005. *Colonialism/Postcolonialism*, 2nd ed. Routledge.

Rivera, Mayra. 2007. *The Touch of Transcendence: A Postcolonial Theology of God*. Westminster John Knox Press.

Ramazani, Jahan. 2001. *The Hybrid Muse: Postcolonial Poetry in English*. The University of Chicago Press.

Sugirtharajah, R. S. 2001. *The Bible and The Third World: Precolonial, Colonial and Postcolonial Encounters*. University Press.

Sugirtharajah, R. S. 1998. *Asian Biblical Hermeneutics and Postcolonialism: Contesting the Interpretations*. Orbis Books.

Young, Robert J. C. 1995. *Colonial Desire: Hybridity in Theory, Culture and Race*. Routledge.

LATINA FEMINIST THEOLOGIES

Like other contextual and liberation theologies, Latin American and *mujerista* theologies begin in lived experiences and struggles for survival of women who are of Latin American descent and the particularities of their oppression at the intersections of race/ethnicity, nation, language, class, sexuality, and gender. Because of the European conquest of the Americas, Latinas' struggles for liberation and Latina theologies cannot be separated from the colonial context in which their lives are shaped, from the European conquest of the Americas that stole lands, resources, cultures, and human lives to the continued exploitations and racism of the present. The consequences of colonialism are grave and far-reaching, and Latinas lives today are still shaped by the intersections of colonialism, sexism, racism, classism, and heterosexism.

Latina feminist theologians also note the extent of the church's complicity with their oppression as racist and patriarchal versions of Christianity have been imposed on Latin America (Tamez 1992). Within this context, Latinas experience both the legacy of white men's devaluing and exploiting of Latinas and Latino machismo and dominance over Latinas in response to their own domination by Europeans. Additionally, the liberation theologies that arose in Latin America ignored women and women's issues in their thinking about socio-economic realities and class oppression. To be useful to Latina liberation, feminist theologies must be a liberative praxis that both explains the material conditions of

DOI: 10.4324/9781032643939-7

Latinas' lives and creates structural changes to ensure Latinas' survival and thriving.

US Latina theologian Michelle Gonzalez points out that Latina feminist theologies arose in the context of other late 20th century development: Latin American liberation theology, feminist theology, feminist critical theory, and US Latino/a theology (2023, 141). Edwin Aponte and Miguel de la Torre add, "U.S. Latina feminist theologies enable Latina women to understand multiple oppressive structures, identify their preferred future, and confront internalized oppression. Furthermore, Latina feminist theologies identify the importance of female leadership, even in the midst of oppression, in maintaining the health and life of the *comunidad*" (2020, 138)

LATINA CONTEXT AND COMMUNITY

To understand Latina theology, we must examine and understand Latinas' particular context and community from which their theology emerges. Many Latinas have common experiences of bilingualism, multiculturalism, and popular religious faith. These experiences are advantageous as they allow them to straddle different contexts and view the world through multiple lenses. Living, as feminist Gloria Anzaldua put it in 1987, "in the borderlands" between nations, cultures, and languages, Latinas draw on their rich, diverse experiences to construct creative and inclusive theologies that help move them toward liberation. Those who are bilingual are able to move between two linguistic spaces that can help them navigate in-between spaces. Different linguistic tones can provide deeper and various contexts for their existence. The ability to move between cultures helps them cultivate a deep sense of the role of culture in shaping their identities, experiences, and theologies.

Puerto Rican feminist theologian, Loida Martell-Otero, points out how Latinas also often share experiences of marginality, poverty, colonization, migration, and cultural alienation (Martell-Otero et al. 2013, 10). One of the ongoing legacies of colonialism is the poverty faced by many Latinas in Latin America and the United States. They often live not only on cultural margins but also economic ones. They often live in colonized places and countries. Colonization disorients them and displaces many of them. This leads many to become migrants or refugees who seek better places to live, and yet they often face hostility and danger as they seek to cross borders, especially into the United States.

Many Latinas are undereducated and are underemployed as a result of systems of sexism and racism that create economic vulnerabilities for Latinas. The likelihood that they are poor is double that of white women. They are often exploited and taken advantage of in the workplace and in their communities. They lack access to quality housing and proper health care which contributes other negative consequences like illnesses, job loss, and poverty. In 1996, Latin American theologian Justo L. González observed that "every negative statistic for Hispanics—employment, underemployment, poverty rate, school dropouts—has remained at a steady 150% of what it has been for the rest of the population" (González 1996, 57). González's observation still holds and is being exacerbated in the present moment by US policies toward Latin American immigrants and refugees.

Additionally, Latinas lack "access to vital connections" (Martell-Otero et al. 2013, 10), the relationships that sustain and advance people in their work, education, and prospects. This lack of connections creates difficulty finding jobs, which could help them climb the economic ladder toward economic success. The lack of connections keeps them in the margins without the important opportunities which are usually afforded to white people.

Latinas are not newcomers to the United States but are rather an intrinsic part of the history of the Americas. They are also an important constituent of the Christian church as they contribute, participate, and are part of the church. They are an estimated half of the Catholic Church membership, and this estimate may also be on the rise. Latinas are not just members within Catholic Churches but are also a growing part of American Protestant churches. It is now estimated that 25 percent of the Latina population is affiliated with some Protestant, evangelical, Pentecostal, or charismatic denomination (Maduro 1996, 151). Therefore they are part of the makeup of Christianity within the United States and are an important part of the theological makeup of the Americas. For many Latinas, their religious faith is intrinsic to their cultural mores and identities (Martell-Otero et al. 2013, 10).

TASKS OF LATINA FEMINIST THEOLOGIES

Latina theology is a grassroots reflection and work which is distinguished by two primary characteristics. First, Latina theology is a distinctive expression of Latina women who live a pluriform and multidimensional existence. This multidimensional existence has been seen as *mestizaje, mulatez,* and *sata/o* ("mongrel"). Each of these terms is helpful to describe Latinas' unique identities, but they are also inadequate and underscore the complex biological, cultural, linguistic, and religious mix which are part of Latina identity. This multifaceted and multidimensional existence leads to a plurality of theologies (Martell-Otero et al. 2013, 10). These diverse theologies offer helpful contributions across feminist theologies in dialogue with experiences and theological reflections of women of other races, ethnicities, and national origins.

Latina women experience pluriformity in their lives, and this in turn affects how they do theology. Pluriformity precludes any singular or univocal description by its very nature and implies an inherent multiplicity as it is an encounter of multiple elements. One finds elements of both Latin American and European theology in any Latina theological formulation as it has a common heritage with these groups. Additionally, this heritage produces a third reality: a new *mestiza* expression that is distinctively Latina (Martell-Otero et al. 2013, 10, 11). This hybrid approach—mixing elements which both remain distinct and create something new—is characteristic of postcolonial feminist theologies, which we explore in Chapter 6.

A key figure in Latina feminist theologies (which she called *"mujerista* theologies"), US Latina feminist theologian Ada Maria Isasi-Díaz, suggested a number of tasks for Latina feminist theologies (1988, 1996, 2004b). The primary task of *mujerista* theology is liberation. For Latinas this is a liberation from both internalized oppression and the oppressive structures of patriarchal society, including the church. Liberation is not an academic idea but rather a necessity to ensure the physical survival of Latinas. Argentinian feminist theologian Nelly Ritchie argues that for a people on a continent "bleeding to death," the need is not for personal salvation but for liberation for all people (1989, 82).

This liberation begins in another of Latina feminist theologies' tasks, the enablement of Latinas through encouragement of their development of a strong sense of moral agency and self-value. This task includes helping Latinas understand the oppressive structures that exercise almost complete control over their daily lives and their own responsibility to change these structures radically so they become life-affirming. To do so, Latina feminist theologies must assist Latinas in affirming that God is in the midst of their communities and intimately involved in their everyday lives.

Latina theology is built on critical reflection based on the day-to-day, or popular, religious beliefs found within the Latina community. It is an integral part of *la vida cotidiana*, which can be translated to "daily" or "everyday" life. What happens on a daily basis affects theological task and interpretations. Isasi-Díaz states that *la vida cotidiana* is what "constitutes the immediate spaces of our lives, the first horizon in which we have our experiences that in turn are constitutive elements of our reality" (Isasi-Díaz 2004c, 95). Latinas' daily lives matter as their lived experiences of oppression and marginalization impact their theological work and journey. If theology does not address these daily concerns, it does not matter or concern Latina women. Theology must tackle their daily issues as they live as multiply marginalized women, subordinated within their own Latin communities and in dominant white society.

Another task of Latina feminist theologies is to name, understand, and challenge the reality of structural sin. Rather than only seeing sin as an individual issue of personal wrong-doing, Latina feminist theologies affirm that sin is also social and structures—that the very institutions, policies, practices, and laws that harm Latinas and threaten their survival are indeed sinful. A single focus on sin as individual obscures the functions of social structures to maintain oppression, thwart the ability of Latinas to survive and flourish, and create destruction and death.

Latina feminist theologies must also encourage Latinas to define their own preferred futures and imagine what a radically changed and life-affirming society would look like. In theological terms, this means Latina feminist theologies must develop an eschatology that is not only focused on a future afterlife but also (and primarily) on a future transformed society in this life. This future, then, can break into Latinas' present-day oppression to inspire them to resist and continue in the struggle toward a different world.

These changes only happen when Latinas can both overcome their own internalized oppression and investment in the very structures that oppress them (church, family, media, government, etc.) and engage in personal and organized resistance. This change begins within each Latina. In theological language, this is the process of conversion, recognizing the realities of oppression and structural sins in their lives and their complicity with it and then refusing to accept their lot and cooperate in their own (and others') oppression.

KEY PRINCIPLES FOR LATINA FEMINIST THEOLOGY

Mexican-born feminist theologian Maria Pilar Aquino enumerates a number of key principles for Latina feminist theology. The first is the centrality of revelation as salvation. Salvation, she says, is "liberation from every oppression" (2002, 151). For Latina theology, liberation from poverty and injustice is "the most effective and credible manifestation of God's salvation." The role of popular religion is another guiding principle. In popular religion, a sense of the sacred pervades everyday life. In the case of Latinas, religious faith has contributed to oppression, and it has propelled Latinas' liberation struggles. Latina feminist theologies, then, must center the religious faith and experiences of everyday Latinas. Latina feminist theologies also draw from liberation theology's principle of God's preferential option for the poor and oppressed. This principle means that God sides with the oppressed over the powerful and calls all people to join in work toward justice. As a transformative practice, Latina feminist theologies strive specifically to transform the systems of oppression that harm women and other minoritized people. It is in these struggles that theology happens as participants experience God at work with them.

Socio-ecclesial equality is a central moral and theological imperative for Latina feminist theologies because Latinas live in a context of intersecting oppressions. Equality and liberation are key goals of Latina feminist theologies, and everyday practices of resistance are the methods and content of Latina feminist theologies (2002, 152–153).

WHO IS GOD FOR LATINAS?

When white missionaries go into new places, they bring the white male God with them. When Latinas and other non-white people have brought their cultures, languages, and traditions to the theological task, the church has often accused them of syncretism, suggesting their adaptations of theological ideas about God arising from their own experiences are misinformed, if not heretical. Of course, European Christians were not immune from syncretism themselves, bringing a new religion that emerged within a Jewish Palestinian context into white European cultures and mixing them with ideas from European paganism and nature-based religions.

Despite resistance from the church, Latinas have still brought transmuted or syncretistic practices into Christian faith and practice. For example, the phrase "Ave María Purísima!" ("Hail Mary most pure!") is a common saying in Puerto Rico. Another example of this transmutation is the evangélica adoption and adaptation of the Free Church or Anabaptist belief in the unmediated presence of God which is made available to every believer. Evangélicas reinterpreted this belief through the lens of a sacramental worldview, which acknowledges God's mediation in the everyday and in the lived lives of Latinas. They also believed that through their Amerindian and African roots, they were able to encounter God without mediation. The various ways of understanding God's mediation influences evangélica ecclesiology, worship, and belief. This Latina understanding of divine mediation contributes to the strong understanding of *presencia* (God's presence), which is experienced by Latina women. Furthermore, a deep focus on the is also emphasized in their theology (Martell-Otero et al. 2013, 11). Latinas do not think God is an old white man sitting on a throne up in the sky, but rather God is present in the everyday lived experiences of Latin women. They experience God in their difficulties and in their loneliness. They understand that God is with them as they seek employment and live the best lives they can. God is with them in their pain and in their joys, and it is God who liberates them.

Latina women emphasize the presence of the Holy Spirit in their Christianity and daily living. The Spirit, rather than God the Father, is the One who not only empowers women but also legitimizes their calling—an important role for those whose voices are often suppressed within patriarchal and racist social and ecclesial structures (Martell-Otero et al. 2013, 12). The spirit empowers Latinas to become ministers and leaders in the church. They do not have to ignore their calling as they believe it is the power of the Spirit which stirs them and moves them into their calling.

There is an affinity for the person and role of the Spirit as one who saves, heals, affirms, calls, empowers, and transforms persons and communities. The Spirit is the subversive One who pours out charisms and enables women as *personas llamadas* (called) to do *trabajo* personal (God's work) in peripheral places where others hesitate to go, because where the Spirit is, there is God. Spirit is evidence that God is present with them always. To be called is to be *sanctificada* (sanctified) and this sense of being "set apart for" includes certain roles patriarchal ecclesial structures have assigned only to men (Martell-Otero et al. 2013, 12). This is an essential aspect of Latina theology, which is an embodied theology that takes Latina bodies and lived experiences seriously. The

Spirit affirms that Latina lives are important and, whatever happens, the Spirit of God is with them and is present in their lives. This focus on the Spirit who saves and heals them is liberating and empowering for women who are oftentimes ignored or marginalized.

CONSTRUCTING A PREFERRED FUTURE

Central to Latina feminist theologies is a vision of the future toward which Latinas are working (Isasi-Díaz 1996). This vision of the future is a radical reimagining of the world toward equity and justice. Such a vision requires a rejection of liberal notions of equality within existing structures because existing structures are themselves oppressive and can never provide true equality. As part of that preferred future, Latinas must refuse to be involved in violence and oppression against other groups. Their liberation cannot be at the expense of another group. Rather, the goal must be to achieve the common good.

In this preferred future, power is not a limited pool of power-over but rather is an unlimited possibility of agency, collaboration, and creativity in which self-determination is respected for all people. Public policy, then, is evaluated in terms of its ability to move the agenda of liberation forward. In the church, oppressive structures must be dismantled and reconstituted to reflect full inclusion, equity, and justice, and people and churches must work together across their differences to make progress toward the common good in the church and in society.

A HOPEFUL UTOPIAN PROJECT

Isasi-Díaz calls this liberatory method a *mujersita proyecto histórico* (2004a), a utopian project that struggles to bring liberation into reality. Utopias, she argues, serve as a way of organizing hopes. They are the hopes and dreams of the oppressed as they understand their daily struggle to survive and work to transform the current situation. This *mujerista* hopeful utopian project draws from desire, hope, feasibility, and pleasure to motivate and sustain the struggle toward liberation.

Desire, Isasi-Díaz says, is what compels people to reach out for what they think is good for them. Desire allows the oppressed to examine their oppression and the material conditions of their lives in a way that moves them from acceptance of their lot in life to a valuing of self and community that directs their action. Desire, "allows our utopian vision to surface" (351). Desire leads to hope, the expectation that something desired can come to be. Hope provides the optimism and energy to work individually and collectively toward social change. Feasibility is the do-ability of the *mujersita proyecto histórico*. Feasibility includes the tools and means to make necessary change. Central to these processes is the belief that life is more than survival, that is also is pleasure and happiness. Latinas must believe they are deserving of fulfilment and material gratification. This fullness of human life includes self-love as well as love of others. The struggle to survive is also a struggle to thrive.

LATINA FEMINIST BIBLICAL INTERPRETATION

For Latinas, the Bible is a key tool both in their oppression and in their liberation. To struggle for liberation and a hopeful utopian project, Latinas must deconstruct oppressive interpretations of the Bible that have contributed to their oppression and offer new readings that are life-affirming and liberatory.

The starting point for Latina feminist biblical interpretation is Latinas' experiences and struggles for survival. Often, Latinas do not have the tools to interpret the Bible and therefore accept authoritative interpretations from church leaders, often to their own detriment. Rather than relying on authorities, Latina feminist interpreters begin in experience and read the Bible in order to further Latina liberation. The Bible's importance for Latinas is not in its role in personal piety or church doctrine but in its usefulness for Latina liberation. Therefore, the Bible becomes part of Latina feminist theologies only as it is needed to further the struggle for liberation.

The critical lens for biblical interpretation for Latinas is liberation-both cultural and physical survival. *Mujerista* interpretation, therefore, is not concerned only with personal salvation; rather, the Bible is used to advance struggle for liberation. In *mujerista* interpretation, the Bible is interpreted through the lens of Latina liberation; it is authoritative only insofar as it supports Latina liberation. The word of God is not the Bible but belief in God's presence in daily struggles.

An example of a Latina feminist interpretation of the Bible comes from Ahida Calderón Pilarski who reads the legal codes of the Pentateuch by beginning with the situation of women farmworkers in the United States. Central to their experience is sexual harassment and assault. Pilarski draws from the Pentateuch's legal codes to explore what the Bible has to say about migrants. She notes that while these passages affirm the dignity of migrants, they do not consider women in the same way. Still, the legal material in the Pentateuch offers a model for centering principles such as dignity in the law and the ongoing reshaping of laws to preserve human dignity (2024, 333).

QUEER LATINA THEOLOGIES

Gloria Anzaldúa claims that the ultimate rebellion for Latinas against their culture is through their sexual behavior (2021, 76). At the intersections of gender, sexuality, race/ethnicity, and religion, Anzaldúa claims, this rebellion is also characterized by fear: "We're afraid of being abandoned by the mother, the culture, la Raza, for being unacceptable, faulty, damaged" (76–77). While this fear leads some Latinas to conform to dominant cultural norms, others face it and embrace the challenge of their sexuality. She writes:

> As a mestizo I have no country, my homeland cast me out; yet all countries are mine because I am every woman's sister or potential lover. (As a lesbian I have no race, my own people disclaim me; but I am all races because there is the queer of me in all races.) I am cultureless because, as a feminist, I challenge the collective cultural/ religious male-derived beliefs of Indo-Hispanics and Anglos; yet

> I am cultured because I am participating in the creation of yet another culture, a new story to explain the world and our participation in it, a new value system with images and symbols that connect us to each other and to the planet.
>
> (2021, 150)

Picking up on Anzaldúa's call for a new culture and story, Argentinian feminist theologian Marcella Althaus-Reid developed an "indecent theology" to create space for queer Latina experience within feminist, liberation, and queer theologies. She writes, "Indecent theology is a theology which problematizes and undresses the mythical layers of multiple oppression in Latin America, a theology which, finding its point of departer at the crossroads of Liberation Theology and Queer Thinking, will reflect on economic and theological oppression with passion and imprudence. An Indecent Theology will question the traditional Latin American field of decency and order as it permeates and support the multiple (ecclesiological, theological, political, and amatory) structures of life in my country, Argentina, and in my continent" (2001, 2).

Despite the work of Anzaldúa and Althaus-Reid, Latina/o theologies have been slow to incorporate explorations of sexuality and desire (Espinoza 2023, 391). The emerging field of *teología de jotería* draws from feminist, queer, and Latin theologies to offer an alternative to single axis theologies that are not intersectional in their approach. Robert Che Espinoza explains the field of *jotería* Studies which has influenced the development of *teología de jotería*. *Jotería* Studies, he writes, is "rooted in the critique of empire and its epistemological standpoint is decolonial, emerging from an intellectual analysis, not simply an appendix including intersectional analysis as the hegemonic center of queer theory suggests. *Jotería* Studies begins with life and looks for the possibilities and another possible future. *Jotería* Studies is a queer counter-story to the LGBTQI+ movement" (398). At this point, Espinoza points out, there are few scholars doing *teología de jotería,* but he sees the discipline is becoming. He sees *teología de jotería* as full of possibilities for a truly decolonial, intersectional theology for Latina/o as it brings voices at the margins of the margins to the center.

BIBLIOGRAPHY

Althaus-Reid, Marcella. 2001. *Indecent Theology: Theological Perspectives in Sex, Gender, and Politics*. Routledge.

Anzaldúa, Gloria. 2021. *Borderlands: La Frontera: The New Mestiza*. Critical Edition. Aunt Lute.

Aquino, Maria Pilar. 2002. "Latina Feminist Theology: Central Features," p. 133–160. In *A Reader in Latina Feminist Theology: Religion and Justice*, Eds. María Pilar Aquino, L. Machado Daisy & Jeanette Rodríguez.

Aponte, Edwin and Miguel de la Torre. 2020. *Introducing Latinx Theologies*. Orbis Books.

Espinoza, Roberto Che. 2023. "Queer Theory and Latinoxa Theologizing," In *The Wiley Blackwell Companion to Latinoax Theology*. Ed. Orlando O. Espin. John Wiley & Sons.

González, Justo L. 1996. *Santa Biblia: The Bible Through Hispanic Eyes*. Abingdon Press.

Gonzalez, Michelle. 2023. "Latina Feminist Theology," p. 136–148. In *Emerging Theologies from the Global South*, Eds. Mitri Raheb & Mark A. Lamport.

Isasi-Díaz, Ada Maria. 1996. *Mujerista Theology*. Orbis Books.

Isasi-Díaz, Ada Maria and Yolanda Tarango. 1988. *Hispanic Women: Prophetic Voice in the Church*. Harper and Row.

Isasi-Díaz, Ada Maria. 2004a. "*Burando Al Opresor*: Mocking/Tricking the Oppressor: Dreams and Hopes of Hispana/Latinas and Mujeristas." *Theological Studies*, 65 (2): 340–363.

Isasi-Díaz, Ada Maria. 2004b. *En La Lucha/In the Struggle: Elaborating a Mujerista Theology*. Fortress Press.

Isasi-Díaz, Ada Maria. 2004c. *La Lucha Continues: Mujerista Theology*. Orbis Books.

Maduro, Otto. 1996. "Notes toward a Sociology of Latina/o Religious Empowerment," In *Hispanic/Latino Theology*. Eds. Ada Maria Isasi-Díaz & Fernanda F. Segovia. Fortress Press.

Martell-Otero, Loida, Zaida Maldonado Prez and Conde-Frazier Elizabeth. 2013. *Latina Evanglicas: A Theological Survey from the Margins*. Cascade Books.

Pilarski, Ahida Calderón. 2024. "Latina and Mujerista Biblical Hermeneutics: A Contribution to Decolonizing the Theme of (Im) migration," p. 319–338. In *The Critic in the World: Essays in Honor of Fernando F. Segovia*. SBL Press.

Ritchie, Nelly. 1989. "Women and Christology," p. 79–91. In *Through Her Eyes: Women's Theology from Latin America*. Ed. Elsa Tamez. Orbis Books.

Tamez, Elsa. 1992. "*Quetzlcoatl y El Dios Cristiano: alianza y lucha de Dioses.*" *Cuadernos de Teolgia y Cultura*, 6: 5–13.

AFRICAN WOMEN'S/ FEMINIST THEOLOGIES[1]

African feminist theologies begin in the context of African women's lives within a continent that has been colonized and, as a result, faces ongoing economic exploitation and political instability. Core to African feminist theologies are women's experiences of dire poverty, patriarchy, and violence. As Ghanian feminist theologian Mercy Oduyoye notes, African women, in response, see themselves as mothers of the continent whose responsibilities include caring for the community, sustaining life, and maintaining culture (2001, 24). African feminist theology, then, reflects the multiple marginalization of African women and their struggles to overcome poverty and oppression on behalf of themselves and all African people.

For African women, cultural beliefs and practices, such as kinship, lineage, and marriage, are powerful factors in everyday life. Oduyoye (2001, 25) argues that since marriage is the practice that moves people into adulthood, marriage is an essential issue for feminist theologians because it is so central in governing lives and communities. Relationships, beginning with the family, are core to Africans' prioritization of community, and African feminist theologies must take into account family and community contexts and must prove life-affirming at all these levels.

Theologizing in the African context also requires weighing the impact of the Christianization of Africa through colonization as well as the presence of people of other religious faiths—Muslims, practitioners of traditional African religions, Buddhists, and others. Patriarchal traditions within all of these faiths have played a significant role in women's subordination across the continent. The dehumanization of Africans in general and African women in particular within colonial systems in which religion has played a significant role has been a key factor in ongoing exploitation. As Batswana feminist biblical critic Muse Dube claims, colonization was done in the name of God, gold, and glory—and she adds a fourth "g," gender (2000, 56).

Colonization has had negative effects on African culture, religion, and spirituality. Colonialism always damages colonized people, and its long-lasting effects can be disastrous. The effects on African women have also been devastating as some theologians note that before Christianity and colonialism arrived in Africa, African women were viewed as having numerous gifts, such as healings, prophecy, and exorcisms, which were exercised voluntarily. These gifts were welcomed by Africans, and women were regarded highly. These gifts that African women shared were embraced in African religion, spirituality, and practice. Prophecy in Africa was and continues to be highly regarded (Maseno 2024, 26), and African women's prophetic role in African religions was significant This high regard for African women's gifts of prophecy was destroyed by Christianity and colonialism.

Furthermore, white missionaries taught African women about gender roles and patriarchy which further reinforced their subordination to men (Mukonyora 2017, 197). When missionaries come in the name of God to teach African women that they are less than men, their teachings carry great power and divine reinforcement, even though these teachings are not true to the gospel message. As white male missionaries traveled to Africa with the "good news" and shared them as divine words to African women, they damaged African women's roles as gifted prophetic leaders. This diminished their personhood, and they became doubly subordinated within patriarchal African culture and colonialism.

African feminist theologians contend with this nexus of oppressive powers, seeking liberation and justice for all people.

While women continue to live in poverty that has resulted from centuries of economic exploitation, their impoverishment is complicated by gender. In many places in Africa, they are still the property of men, and their lives are controlled by men. As the people responsible for caring for children, they are more vulnerable to economic pressures. Even international aid programs often overlook them because these programs are run by Westerners who project their notions of gender onto African women. Christian missionaries also have brought ideas about women's submission and silence to Africa, and churches, which should be liberatory spaces, often simply cement women's subordination through their teachings and practices.

Nigerian feminist theologian Rosemary Edet and Kenyan feminist theologian Bette Ekeya argue that the task for African women's theology is to reclaim the heritage of African women in traditional religions and grassroots Christianity. They add that African women's theologizing must include the stories and thinking of all African women, whether they be formally educated as theologians or not. "There is not a single African woman's experience of life in church and society that the theologian can afford to ignore," they declare (1988, 12).

STORYTELLING IN AFRICAN FEMINIST THEOLOGIES

Storytelling is central to African societies, and, in places where large numbers of women are functionally illiterate, storytelling plays a key role in analyzing and understanding the world. Also, in many African communities, storytelling is mostly done by women, and it is a form that is accessible to both educated and uneducated women. Storytelling, then, is a primary methodology of African feminist theologies and African feminist biblical interpretation. For African feminist theologians and biblical critics, these stories of everyday women are the starting place for theology and interpretation, and theology and interpretation must return to improve the lives of these everyday women at their center.

Traditional stories, too, must be part of African feminist theologizing. Musa Dube (2001, 3) points out that many characteristics of African stories make them especially useful as hermeneutics for empowering women: many stories are gender-neutral (feature animals); and many feature "flat" characters that are tricksters who represent values and philosophies of survival (such as Spider in western Africa)—small individuals among big and powerful animals.

South African Biblical critic Mmadipoane Masenya (2001, 148–149) offers what she calls a *bosadi* (womanhood) approach to African women's liberation. She lists five important elements of this approach:

1. A critique of oppressive elements that constrain and harm Africa women alongside a reclaiming of aspects of culture that empower women;
2. A critique of the oppressive elements of the Bible and an explication of the liberative elements;
3. Attention to the intersections of post-apartheid racism, sexism, classism, and African culture at play in the lives of African women;
4. Centrality of the concept of *botho/ubuntu*–"I am because we are" and "We are because I am." This African idea recognizes the interplay of individual and community and acknowledges that liberation is a community/collective commitment/activity;
5. Focus on the significance of family for Africans. Masenya argues, "Sick families give birth to sick societies, and the latter breeds a sick world." For her, that means any liberatory theology must strengthen the family even as it works toward liberation for women.

African feminist theology cannot be removed from the everyday lives of women, their families, and their communities, and so African feminist theologians often engage in conversations with everyday women to construct theologies of liberation. Because the Bible is a key feature of African Christians' lives, African feminist theologies must also take the Bible into account and incorporate its reading into theologies. Its stories must be in dialogue with African women's stories for it to be useful in African women's liberation.

Storytelling is powerful and compelling as it turns the culturally invisible, embodied experience into audible words and stories. Storytelling serves as a vital means of preserving and passing down traditions, values, and ways of life—offering a source of strength and connection, particularly for many African women. It breathes life into histories, rituals, and familial legacies, ensuring they are shared with the wider community and passed on to future generations.

Storytelling is a source of healing, liberation, and empowerment, making it a vital element of African women's theology. It has the power to create subversive memory, inspiring women to advocate for justice. By shedding light on women's experiences—often overlooked, dismissed, or rendered invisible by patriarchal structures—storytelling challenges dominant narratives. African women's theology has also used feminist theology from the West as a source for theology. Western feminist theology has been adapted because it challenges cultural socialization and rejects the assumption of inherent and God-ordained gender roles. African women theologians have adapted, modified and reworked some of western feminist theologies to address their specific African context of colonization and oppression. They have also applied African and western feminist methods to their reading of the Bible.

AFRICAN FEMINIST BIBLICAL INTERPRETATION

Musa Dube begins her practice of African feminist biblical criticism by "reading with" and "reading from" Black, non-academic readers. She uses the term "ordinary readers" to include most women outside academia who also hold suppressed knowledges that are useful in liberatory readings of the Bible. Dube "reads with" non-academic African women to subvert dominant Western and patriarchal discourses by including different interpretive communities. She "reads from" non-academic readers by learning from their strategies of interpretation born from struggles with imperialism and sexism (2001, 8–9).

Kenyan theologian Musimbi Kanyoro (2001, 101) uses the term "cultural hermeneutics" to describe "reading with." It involves critical analysis of one's own Black African culture alongside critical engagement with the Bible. Cultural hermeneutics requires feminist biblical readers to recognize the ways culture implicitly shapes interpretation and the usefulness of readings of the Bible for African women. For example, Kanyoro explains that feminist theories rooting oppression in men as oppressors are not useful tools for African women because it threatens solidarity among African women, many of whom see these theories as a danger to community. Rather, she argues, theologies and readings of the Bible must make room for the breadth and depth of human experience and cultures to move toward a truly inclusive and liberating praxis. Another Kenyan theologian, Loreen Maseno, points out that in African feminist theologies, "women work in cooperation with men of good will for the reconstruction of a cultural and religious praxis of equality," even while critiquing women's subordination within patriarchy in Africa (2021, 5).

Dube adds that African feminist readings of the Bible must also be postcolonial. African women's experience has been indelibly shaped by Western imperialism and its colonizing structures that affect every aspect of African women's daily lives. Dube recognizes that Christianity in general and its uses of the Bible in particular have played a key role in the advance of imperialism and the subordination of Africa. The colonial enterprise, for Dube, has been to take Africa's lands and resources and impose Western notions and structures on the continent. For her, women have often been overlooked both by white colonizers and Black postcolonial thinkers. She says a liberatory reading of the Bible must take both imperialism and patriarchy seriously (2000, 23).

This includes critiquing the colonial entanglements of the text itself, those places in the text where the Bible justifies the taking of other people's lands and resources, and the ways the text has been used by the church and the missionary enterprise in particular to support colonial invasions of Africa and the plundering of Africa's resources by the West. Within those critiques, readers must also pay attention to the ways gender operates and how imperialism and patriarchy reinforce one another in the lives of Africa's women. Finally, a liberatory postcolonial feminist reading must seek those places in the text that offer encouragement and empowerment to African women to challenge their subordination with patriarchal imperialism and demand equity within transformed African societies.

HEARTH-HOLD AND HOSPITALITY

Mercy Oduyoye (2001, 78) centers African feminist theologies in cultural practices of welcome and hospitality. She notes that home-making is a primary activity for African women, and therefore theological reflection must take into account women's household roles and their connections with relationships with others and with God. She draws on Nigerian sociologist Felicia I. Ekejuiba to suggest rather than using the term "household" to talk about the home setting for African women we use the word "hearth-hold." Ekejuiba contends that African communities are organized around the hearth-holds of women, and so the church must be the hearth-hold of God.

Hospitality is encouraged in Africa, and this is true in the church. African women often view hospitality as the mark of divinity and therefore something which human beings should practice (Maseno 2024, 28, 29). Hospitality is integrated into the life of the church where everyone is welcomed, and foreigners are shown what it means to be part of their communities.

Hospitality is a profound celebration and embodiment of the Christ—it is, at its core, about embracing the other. In Christian tradition, the theological concept of *perichoresis* (meaning "mutual indwelling") reflects the relationship within the Holy Trinity and God's embrace of humanity through the cross. Just as God welcomes us through this divine act of love, we are called to extend that same embrace to one another. Hospitality has become a fundamental African cultural value (Assefa & Belachew 2024, 51). The power of hospitality challenges the West also to adapt it as a central part of theology Christian practice.

African women have come to understand that love overcomes the sin of fear, exclusion, and alienation. Hospitality, therefore, becomes a profound acknowledgment of the image of God in others, transcending differences of ethnicity and gender. The well-known African concept of *Ubuntu*—"I am because we are"—reflects this deep interconnectedness. The mystery of humanity lies in recognizing God's presence in others and granting them the respect and dignity they deserve, as if seeing the Creator. Hospitality thus becomes a sacred dialogue—an expression of understanding, respect, recognition, love, and the wholehearted embrace of the other (Assefa & Belachew 2024, 51). It becomes an important practice which urges the rest of the world also to practice it so that we can seek kindness, love and understanding which welcome the stranger, who is God.

For African women, hospitality is a key characteristic of the hearth-hold. Particularly in the midst of the horrors of colonialism and sexism and their attendant violence and degradation, hospitality becomes a practice of spirituality for African women, a way to preserve and improve life. In particular, hospitality is an openness to the "other," the visitor who needs shelter, food, and healing. In African feminist theologies, God is also one of these visitors who is welcomed into the hearth-hold. Hospitality, especially in its concrete and material forms, is a bulwark against the ravages of colonialism and its resultant economic ravages. For African feminist theologians, economic and spiritual problems are related and must be solved together.

African feminist theologians also recognize that hospitality can be taken advantage of, especially within the context of patriarchy. Women's hospitality can be perverted into subservience and submission, with greater burdens of responsibility for the labor of daily family and community life falling on women. Women's sexuality can also be exploited through individual and structural practices of sexism that use women as objects of transactions between men. African feminist theologies denounce the exploitation of African women's labor and bodies and call for hospitality toward, as well as from, African women.

Salvation, then, for African women must include a rejection of self-sacrifice and an acceptance of God's redeeming work as the one who suffers with and empowers African women to liberate themselves from death-dealing structures of colonialism and patriarchy. African feminist theologies also call the church to work toward the liberation of African women by rejecting their exploitation and subjugation and working toward inclusion and justice.

HIV/AIDS, WOMEN, AND AFRICAN FEMINIST THEOLOGY

A central concern for African feminist theologians for the past four decades has been the impact of HIV/AIDS on African women, men, families, and communities. HIV/AIDS was already an epidemic in Africa among heterosexual men and women before it was first identified primarily among gay men in the United States in the 1980s, and, despite medical gains against the disease, it continues to ravage sub-Saharan Africa with particular impact on women. Theologies by African feminists recognize that the devastation of HIV/AIDS is a key theological question

Nearly 40 million people worldwide are living with HIV/AIDS, more than half of them women, more than half of them in eastern and southern Africa. Over 1 million were newly infected in the past year. In sub-Saharan Africa, women and girls accounted for 62% of all new HIV infections. Every week in sub-Saharan Africa, 3,100 girls and young women between 15 and 24 years old become infected (UN AIDS 2024). In 2023, more than 600,000 people worldwide died of HIV/AIDS-related complications.

For African feminist theologians, their tasks have been to challenge stigma related to HIV/AIDS status, especially the idea that infection is a punishment for sin, to develop inclusive theologies of sexuality and safe sex, to educate about the disease, to foster compassion, and to encourage understandings of healing and wholeness in the face of the pandemic. In particular, feminist theologians must examine reasons women are culturally and socially more vulnerable to infection and to worse health outcomes and urge responses on every level to provide prevention and care. African feminist theologians also call for liturgies to help the church address the pandemic and offer care and support for those affected by it (Oduyoye 2019).

The HIV/AIDS pandemic in Africa has created an acute theological crisis, raising the question of why people suffer and what kind of God has allowed or sent the suffering that comes in the wake of HIV/AIDS. African feminist theologians have responded by challenging the church to see HIV/AIDS as more than a medical issue. Isabel Apawo Phiri suggests the pandemic has called the church to rethink how it sees itself as "having been sent by God to bring wholeness to a broken world" (2010, 223). She argues that the church must move away from seeing HIV/AIDS as sent by God as a punishment for sin to seeing God as in solidarity with people infected by HIV/AIDS.

AFRICAN WOMEN'S CHRIST

For African women, Christ is the "Jesus who saves, the one who not only announced, but also brings and lives good news" (Oduyoye 2001, 57). As Oduyoye notes (2010, 171), African women's theology is almost always focused on Jesus rather than "Christ." Their concerns are material and historical, and they are less concerned with Christological questions than the healing and liberation that come in the person of Jesus. For them, the Christ of history plays a much more important role than the Christ of dogma.

Because of the immense suffering of African women, Christology must be rooted in a Jesus who is a victor over suffering. Jesus both suffers with and overcomes suffering for African women. The Christ of African women must be able to heal individuals and the world. This Christ is a midwife who births a new world and also "questions world structures that impoverish Africa and lie at the heart of much of its suffering" (Isherwood 2002, 97).

For African women, Jesus is also a liberator from misogyny and the subjugation of women. By embracing the human Jesus, African women affirm their own bodies and humanities, claiming the human and divine in Jesus and in themselves. As Louise Tappa explains, "I am convinced that Jesus died so that the patriarchal God might die and that Jesus rose so that the true God revealed in Jesus might rise in our lives, and in our communities" (1988, 31). Loreen Maseno (2024, 33) concludes, "any relevant Christology for African women is one which presents Christ as a concrete and personal figure who engenders hope in the oppressed by siding with women."

African women's Christology is not focused on analyzing the nature of Christ, as was the aim of historical Church Councils that debated Jesus' humanity, divinity, or human-divine nature. Instead, it seeks to identify the saving acts of Jesus that offer African women hope for liberation. Jesus is understood as a liberating Savior, one who actively redeems and uplifts African women. Moreover, Christology becomes a celebration of victories over oppression and death, attributing these triumphs to Jesus rather than to earthly or human authorities (Maseno 2024, 28). African women seek to understand the source of the hope that some have found, ultimately recognizing it as coming from Jesus, their Savior and Liberator. This realization deepens their sense of hope and strengthens their path to liberation, especially in times of struggle and hardship. In embracing Jesus as the source of renewal, African women find the resilience to persevere and reclaim their dignity in the face of adversity.

For African women, Jesus, as revealed in the Scriptures, is a prophetic figure who speaks to the oppressed, the poor, and the sick. Just as many African women possessed the gift of prophecy long before the arrival of white missionaries, they recognize Jesus as a prophet who embodies this same divine calling. Many African women living on the margins of society see their own struggles reflected in Jesus' ministry and find hope and liberation in the salvation he offers (Mukonyora 2017, 202). Jesus is the great Liberator, offering freedom to African women from the many forms of oppression and marginalization they endure. His message of justice, dignity, and love empowers them to reclaim their agency, find hope in their struggles, and embrace the fullness of their humanity.

QUEER AFRICAN FEMINIST THEOLOGIES

Addressing issues of queer sexualities has been complicated in African thought because many within African churches reject queerness as a Western issue or embrace the conservative church's rejection of queer sexuality as inherently sinful. In reality, Christianity and colonialism brought homophobia to Africa. Queerness is seen as un-African and un-Christian (Ngong, n.d.). Queerness is considered un-African because an African focus on procreation to counter the destruction of colonialism places value on child-bearing within the family, and the expectation is that queer people do not reproduce. It is considered unchristian because of interpretations of the Bible that situate queerness as an abomination. Nonetheless, in recent years, African theologians have begun to develop queer theologies that embrace queer people as part of the community and God's kin-dom.

Mercy Oduyoye (1993) criticized theologies that have embraced cultural norms demonizing queer sexualities by normalizing heterosexual relationships geared toward procreation. She sees the equation of sexuality with procreation for women as yet another oppressive form of objectification of women's bodies and identification of womanhood with motherhood. Isabel Phiri (2006) has also identified same-sex relationships between women *sangomas* (traditional healers) in South Africa and argues that their same-sex relationships suggest that same-sex relationships in Africa are not simply an import from the West. In her work on HIV/AIDS, Musa Dube (2008) has gone even further to align queer liberation with struggles against poverty, gender injustice, and colonialism. She contends that liberatory movements must be focused on structural injustices rather than individual sexual morality. She appeals to creation as an affirmation that all life is sacred, regardless of differences, including sexual identities. While the numbers of African theologians affirming queer sexualities remains small, these dissident voices suggest that some theologians are beginning to work toward a more inclusive Christianity in Africa, and, while work remains to be done, their contributions challenge ideas of a monolithic African theological understanding of sexuality and offer hope of discussions that move forward struggles for justice for queer people in Africa (van Klinken and Gunda 2012).

AFRICAN WOMEN AND THE EARTH

African women are attached to the Earth and understand their interconnectedness with the Earth. They have cared for the Earth in ways that Western and industrial women have not, and their theologies remind us that all of us need to be attached to the Earth if we are to prevent the impending ecological crisis. We looked at ecofeminist theologies in Chapter 5. African women's theologies complicate that discussion and bring new perspectives to thinking about the impacts of climate change and the need to care for the Earth. Kenyan ecofeminist Wangari Maathai (2009) often criticized Christianity for its complicity with colonialism and colonialism's destructive impact on the environment. As an activist, however, she also drew on her Catholic faith and the Bible to facilitate environmental awareness and encourage others to work to stop environmental degradation and repair the Earth.

One way many African women practice a deep relationship with the Earth is through burying the umbilical cord after giving birth. This burial provides a strong connection to the Earth through concrete action. Just as the umbilical cord connects the baby to the mother for the baby's sustenance and survival while in the mother's womb, similarly, the burying of the umbilical cord connects the baby to Mother Earth. (Many feminists, however, question the use of the Mother Earth metaphor because it reinforces stereotypical notions of women and their connection to the Earth through their bodies.) This link emphasizes belonging and sustenance for life (Moyo 2017, 179). The lifelong connection of our bodies to the Earth underlines ecofeminist understandings of the unity of nature and the materiality of God in the Earth. If, as Sallie McFague suggests, we imagine the Earth as God's body, we may be compelled to stop harming and to work toward saving the Earth. Seeing the Earth as the Body of God moves us to recognize that God is around us and with us, and in us here on Earth. Therefore, we must do the work to save the Earth. Similarly, African women's theology, which provides a straight connection of self to the Earth by burying the umbilical cord, shows a concrete and positive way of connecting to the Earth and to all the beauty of God's creation.

The practice of umbilical cord burying demonstrates how women not only mother their babies but also co-mother with the Earth. Women are viewed as intermediaries and guardians of Mother Earth (Moyo 2017, 181), and thus their roles are vital to the saving of the Earth. Women are to help protect and sustain the Earth just as they protect and sustain their young and their family. Understanding women as guardians of the Earth challenges patriarchal constructions of women and elevates women in their crucial role in the ongoing life of the Earth.

African women embrace a kenotic ecological theology to understand the relationship between humanity and the Earth. African women desire a praxis-oriented ecological theology (Eppinger 2011, 47). This theology moves away from hierarchical and patriarchal views of nature and humanity and moves toward an understanding of creation that is rooted in ecological justice. It moves toward valuing everyone and everything in creation as important and interconnected. Humans need each other and must care for each other and the Earth, as we cannot live separate from the other parts of creation. What happens to the animals, or our neighbors also impacts us in various ways. The interconnectedness of all of creation is uplifted and emphasized by African women. This view offers a challenge for Western women who often forget this interconnectedness or embrace individualism over the community.

Kenotic theology focuses on the self-emptying God who became human to build a lifegiving and just communion with creation (Moyo 2017, 191). *Kenosis* comes from the Greek word for "emptying." The self-emptying of Jesus' will was voluntary as he "emptied himself, by taking the form of a servant, being born in the likeness of men" (Philippians 2:7).

Therefore, Jesus' humanity was real and thus Jesus experienced human emotions, feelings, and limitations. Jesus became receptive to God and God's will which is how the incarnation came to be. As Jesus came into the world, Jesus demonstrated the way to live justly with all of creation. Within this incarnational theology, Jesus gave up divinity to become human. Likewise, humans may also need to give things up to sustain life for the planet—greed, lust for power, riches, consumption. A kenotic theology challenges people with more resources to give up some of those resources so that everyone can have enough.

The African woman's baby's umbilical cord is buried in the Earth reminding us of the interconnectedness and interdependence of humanity with the Earth. Mother Earth becomes part of our flesh and blood, and we exist in her body (Moyo 2017, 191). We become interdependent with the Earth for our survival and flourishing. As the sacredness of the life of a baby should be revered and honored and respected, so should the sacredness of all of life and the Earth itself.

AFRICAN WOMEN AND MOTHERHOOD

To fight patriarchy from within their own culture as well as colonial power, African women's theology finds liberation in focusing on Mary the God bearer and African women's own motherhood. African women theologians have developed a doctrine of the mother of Christ as a way to fight climate change as it brings together the concept of salvation for the poor as well as saving the Earth (Mukonyora 2017, 197).

Christ having a mother is not unfamiliar to anyone aware of ancient myths of creation. Ancient myths of creation combine male and female imagery in their accounts of the origins of life (Ranger 2007, 87). In the Bible's first creation account, the Spirit that hovers over the deep is female. In many myths, gods have mothers, and so the preeminence of the mother of Jesus is a liberatory and empowering aspect of African women's theology.

The image of Mary as the "Womb of God" is a powerful image of Mary's status and power within the divine (Mukonyora

2017, 203). Her body becomes elevated to hold God within her body. This understanding is not often embraced within Protestant churches. But African women's theology recognizes its life-affirming power for women. Because a woman carried God in her womb, women should be valued rather than subordinated in society and in the church.

For African women's theologies, the ordinary in everyday women's lives is at the center of understanding God and acting in the world. These theologies value the experiences of some of the poorest people in the world and remind that God calls for the social, political, economic, and religious liberation of even "the least of these." As Mercy Oduyoye explains, "Mending broken relations between races, ethnic groups, and faith communities, and embracing the existence of diverse sexual orientations, calls for establishing mutuality and recognizing the joy in the rich diversity of humanity" (2019, 106).

NOTE

1. The term for theologies by and for women coming out of Africa is contested. Many theologians have used the term "African women's theologies" as a way to connect theologies to the majority of African women who would not identify as feminist nor see feminism as relevant in an African context. Other theologians have embraced "African feminist theologies," drawing from Western feminist ideas and creating their own forms of feminist thought specific to their cultures. This chapter uses "African feminist theologies" to align with practice in other chapters in the book.

BIBLIOGRAPHY

Assefa, Daniel and Tekletsadik Belachew. 2024. "Revisiting and Re-Membering the Queen of Sheba: The Daughter of Wisdom, Thirsty for Wisdom," In *Queen of Sheba: East and Central African Women's Theologies of Liberation* (Circle Jubilee Volume 2), Eds. Loreen Maseno, Esther Mombo & Nagaju Muke, u. a. (Hrsg.). University of Bamberg Press.

Dube, Musa. 2000. *Postcolonial Feminist Interpretation of the Bible*. Chalice.

Dube, Musa. 2001. "Introduction," p. 1–19. In *Other Ways of Reading: African Women and the Bible*. Ed. Musa Dube. Society of Biblical Literature.

Dube, Musa. 2008. *The HIV & AIDS Bible: Selected Essays*. University of Scranton Press.

Edet, Rosemary and Bette Ekeya. 1988. "Church Women of Africa: A Theological Community," In *With Passion and Compassion: Third World Women Doing Theology*, Eds. Virginia Fabella & Mercy Amba Oduyoye. Wipf and Stock.

Eppinger, Priscilla E. 2011. "Christian Ecofeminism as Kenotic Ecology: Transforming Relationships Away from Environmental Stewardship." *Journal for the Study of Religion*, 24 (2): 47–63.

Isherwood, Lisa. 2002. *Introducing Feminist Christologies*. Pilgrim Press.

Kanyoro, Musimbi R. A. 2001. "Cultural Hermeneutics: An African Contribution," p. 101–113. In *Other Ways of Reading: African Women and the Bible*, Ed. Musa Dube. Society of Biblical Literature.

Maathai, Wangari. 2009. *The Challenge for Africa*. Pantheon Press.

Maseno, Loreen. 2021. "African Women's Theology and the Re-Imagining of Community in Africa." *HTS Teologiese Studies/Theological Studies*, 77 (2): a6736. https://doi.org/10.4102/hts.v77i2.6736

Maseno, Loreen 2024. "Mapping East and Central African Feminist Theologies," p. 23–40. In *Queen of Sheba: East and Central African Women's Theologies of Liberation* (Circle Jubilee Volume 2), Eds. Eds. Loreen Maseno, Esther Mombo & Nagaju Muke, u. a. (Hrsg.). University of Bamberg Press. https://www.academia.edu/129117122/Mapping_East_and_Central_African_Feminist_Theologies

Masenya, Mmadipoane. 2001. "A *Bosadi* (Womanhood) Reading of Proverbs 31: 1 0-31," p. 145–157. In *Other Ways of Reading: African Women and the Bible*, Ed. Musa Dube. Society of Biblical Literature.

Moyo, Fulata Lusungu. 2017. "'*Ukugqiba Inkaba*'-Burying the Umbilical Cord: An African Indigenous Ecofeminist Perspective on Incarnation," p. 179–192. In *Planetary Solidarity*, Eds. Grace Ji-Sun Kim & Hilda Koster. Fortress Press.

Mukonyora, Isabel. 2017. "Motherhood and Christ in an African Ecofeminist Theology for Climate Justice," p. 192–206. In *Planetary Solidarity*, Eds. Grace Ji-Sun Kim & Hilda Koster. Fortress Press.

Ngong, David. n.d. "Theology in Africa." https://www.saet.ac.uk/Christianity/TheologyinAfrica/1000.pdf.pdf.pdf. Accessed February 18, 2025.

Oduyoye, Mercy Amba. 1993. "A Critique of Mbiti's View on Love and Marriage in Africa," p. 241–366. In *Religious Plurality in Africa. Essays in Honour of John S. Mbiti*, Eds. J. K. Olupona & S. S. Nyang.

Oduyoye, Mercy Amba. 2001. *Introducing African Women's Theology*. Pilgrim Press.

Oduyoye, Mercy Amba. 2019. *African Women's Theologies, Spirituality, and Healing: Theological Perspectives from the Circle of Concerned African Women Theologians*. Paulist Press.

Phiri, Isabel Apawo. 2006. "Dealing With the Trauma of Sexual Abuse: A Gender-Based Analysis of the Testimonies of Female Traditional Healers in KwaZulu-Natal," p. 113–130. In *African Women, Religion and Health. Essays in Honor of Mercy Amba Ewudziwa Oduyoye*, Eds. Isabel Apawo Phiri & S. Nadar. Orbis Books.

Phiri, Isabel Apawo. 2010. "HIV/AIDS: An African Theological Response in Mission," p. 219–228. In *Hope Abundant: Third World Women and Indigenous Women's Theology*, Ed. Kwok Pui-Lan.

Ranger, Shelagh. 2007. *The Word of Wisdom and the Creation of Animals in Africa*. James Clarke.

Tappa, Louise. 1988. "The Christ-Event: A Protestant Perspective," p. 30–34. In *With Passion and Compassion: Third World Women Doing Theology*, Eds. Virginia Fabella & Mercy Amba Oduyoye. Wipf and Stock.

UN AIDS. Fact Sheet 2024. Global HIV Statistics. https://www.unaids.org/sites/default/files/media_asset/UNAIDS_FactSheet_en.pdf. Accessed February 18, 2025.

van Klinken, Adriaan S. and Gunda Masiiwa Ragies. 2012. "Taking Up the Cudgels Against Gay Rights? Trends and Trajectories in African Christian Theologies on Homosexuality." *Journal of Homosexuality* 59:1, 114–138.

QUEER FEMINIST THEOLOGIES

Queer was originally a pejorative term use to harm and oppress LGBTQI+ people, but it has been reclaimed by much of the community as a way to resist its linguistic violence and instead offer an in-your-face affirmation of non-heteronormative sexuality and gender. While terms like gay, lesbian, and bisexual reflect a gender binary —men and women/male and female—queer recognizes the fluidity of gender and sexuality. Queer is what is at odds with the "normal," and, as a practice, queering means disrupting norms, refusing heteronormativity and assumptions of heterosexuality, and challenging essentialist and fixed notions of gender and sexuality.

Queer theory emerges as a vital framework for dismantling the oppressive systems that inscribe themselves upon bodies—systems that regulate, discipline, and define life through normative constructions of gender and sexuality. Recognizing that gender and sexuality are not neutral or innate, but rather political constructs and instruments of power, queer theory exposes how these categories sustain broader structures of domination. Queer feminist theology builds on this and offers a radical theological counterpoint. It constructs a critical, counter-sexual hermeneutic that challenges the authority of classical theologies rooted in cis-heteropatriarchal assumptions. These dominant theological traditions have historically erased or marginalized queer and feminist bodies, reinforcing theological imaginaries shaped by power and control. By centering queer and feminist experiences, queer feminist theology seeks liberation from the theological paradigms—systems that regulate reproduction, sexuality, and identity under the guise of divine order (Contreras, 2024). Queer feminist theology, then, is not merely a critique—it is a constructive and emancipatory project. It reimagines theology through the lens of bodies that have been excluded and rendered invisible and opens space for divine encounters that are embodied, intersectional, and liberative. It creates a deeper engagement with the sacred that honors the full spectrum of human diversity.

Queering theology is a process of challenging the ways theologies reinforce heteronormativity and heterosexual dominance and offering disruptive and inclusive theologies that make room for diverse genders and sexualities. Before queer theologies, lesbian and gay theologies worked to make arguments from fairly traditional theologies for lesbian and gay inclusion rather than condemnation. Queer theologies go far beyond lesbian and gay theologies to upend the very structures of power within theology and the church that maintain the gender binary to offer theologies that make room for and welcome the fluid, ambiguous, and unknown in both the human and the divine.[1]

Like queer theories, however, queer theologies have often been done from the perspectives of men and have overlooked the impacts of sexism and misogyny, particularly on women and female-identifying queer people. Queer theologies have also often been dominated by whiteness and have not been fully intersectional. In response, queer feminist theologies recognize and highlight the ways intersections of sexuality with gender, race/ethnicity, social class, and other forms of social difference contribute to human experience and more inclusive theologies.

Queer theologies are grounded in the body, affirming the body and sexuality. In fact, they move sexuality to the center of theology, contending that sexuality informs every aspect of human experience and so must be central to theologizing. Instead of focusing on a spirituality (or a God, for that matter) that is only spiritual and far-removed from the material, queer theologies celebrate physicality and materiality with sexuality as a primary expression of both humanity and divinity. Thus, in queer theologies, love is not some desexualized abstract concept. Rather love is lived and expressed through bodies, especially through sexuality.

Historically, patriarchy has created binaries between the body and mind or body and spirit and has associated men with mind/spirit and women with the body. This association of women with the body has been used as a justification for women's subordination. Queer theologies' reclaiming of the body and sexuality as essential sites for theologizing is especially important and fruitful for queer feminist theologies that recognize the liberating potential for all women as well as queer people in affirming the body and sexuality as positive and necessary facets of liberatory theologies.

Queer feminist theologies also attend to issues of power, particularly in relation to gender and sexuality, with an intersectional lens. Central to this process are social relations and the ways power is distributed through practices that are gendered and racialized. Queer feminist theologies both analyze the current discourses of theology and suggest new and alternative possibilities for more just discourses and practices. Relatedly, queer feminist theologies also look for resistances to dominant discourses and practices and highlight new ways of being and acting that can bring about a more inclusive, equitable, and just world.

TASKS OF QUEER FEMINIST THEOLOGIES

The first task of queer feminist theologies is to disrupt normative theologies. This begins by challenging traditional heteronormative and binary theologies that rely on stereotypical assumptions of gender and sexuality. For example, queer feminist theologians question theologies of human nature that assume people are either men or women, male or female, and they contest assumptions of Jesus' heterosexuality. One key way queer feminist theologians do this is by bringing subaltern voices and theologies to the surface and ensuring they become a significant part of theological discourse.

Queer feminist theologians also challenge the fixed nature of theological categories, especially those that rely on notion of gender and sexuality as inherent, essential, and inevitable. Instead, they create spaces for diverse, ambiguous, and tentative identities that can offer transformative ways of thinking about and practicing faith. As an intersectional practice, queer feminist theologies also engage in working to decolonize personal identities as well as linguistic categories of gender and sexuality and institutional practices that reinforce fixed and binary genders and sexualities. Queer feminist theologies integrate issues of race/ethnicity, social class, ability, age, and nation into their theological methods and call for people to liberate themselves from the constraints of their own binary and non-intersectional thinking.

Another key way queer feminist theologies challenge heteronormative theologies is through de-familiarizing accepted norms. So, for example, queer feminist theologians explore notions of the queer Christ or the transgender God or ask us to think of God's community as a queer bar instead of a church. These unexpected images shock and demand that we look at the world differently. Queer feminist theologians often use the metaphor of "coming out" as a way to center queer experience and depart from dominant interpretations.

Queer feminist theology emerges from the lived realities of bodies shaped by intersecting systems of control over life, sexuality, and identity. Rooted in resistance and resilience, it reflects the hybridized experiences of those who exist outside normative frameworks. Recognizing that the body is not neutral but constructed through social, political, and religious mechanisms, queer feminist theology becomes a reflective and theological engagement with God—one grounded in the embodied experiences of queer feminist lives (Contreras 2004). Just as feminist theology, emerging in the 1960s, grounded itself in the lived experiences of women, queer theology must also center the lived realities of what it means to be queer in a dominant society. It must address the marginalization, oppression, and suffering that come with being queer—particularly within social spaces, workplaces, and faith communities that may not welcome queer bodies. As such, queer theology becomes biographical: a theology rooted in the body, where queer individuals encounter the divine through their embodied experiences and daily struggles.

Queer feminist theologies form a critical framework that challenges the dominance of cis-heteronormative and patriarchal theological traditions. Rooted in both queer theory and the broader field of sexual theories that began to emerge in the late nineteenth century, these theologies engage with systems of knowledge and practice that resist hegemonic norms (Contreras 2004). They offer a transformative lens through which theology can be reimagined in more inclusive, liberating, and justice-centered ways.

Queer theologies are also intersectional, recognizing that queer bodies also differ by race, ability, age, and gender. Susannah Cornwall points out that while the genealogy of queer theologies begins in Western and white gay and lesbian theologies, queer theologies are not inherently white and Western (2011, 105). Rather, many queer theologies begin in the intersectional experiences of queer people of color in the West and queer people in the Global South. For example queer womanist theologian Pamela Lightsey reminds that Black LGBTQI+ people cannot afford to engage in deconstructing gender and abolishing normative sex categories in the same way white queer people can. She notes that to do so "without attention to the ways in which black bodies as racially identified have been assaulted is to risk aligning ourselves with historic white privileging" (2015, 32). Asian feminist theologian Sharon Bong challenges traditional notions of womanhood, motherhood, and heterosexuality by appealing to images of the lesbian mother and the lesbian nun (2007). Intersectional approaches themselves are queer as they challenge the norms of white, cis, heteropatriarchal dominance. To offer queer theologies only from white queer perspectives reinscribes white dominance while ignoring the multiple and diverse ways race and other social differences impact queerness. Recognizing the contributions of early white gay and lesbian theologies is important, but queer theologies must take into account the intersectional nature of identities and oppressions in order to capture the incredible diversity of queer people across the world.

CHURCH SACRAMENTS

The body of Christ is queer (Stuart 2007, 66), as it challenges normative assumptions about embodiment, identity, and belonging. In the sacraments, particularly the Eucharist, the body of Christ is given to Christians not as a singular, fixed entity but as a body broken, remembered, and shared. Christians practice the sacraments that transcend normative understandings of wholeness, gender, and sexuality. The Eucharistic body is fluid, transformative, and radically inclusive. It resists the binaries that define who is worthy and who is not, who belongs and who does not. The sacraments become grounded in the queer nature of Christ's own body which defied purity laws, crossed boundaries, embraced the outcast, and ultimately disrupted death. The sacramental body invites everyone into communion through grace and love rather than conformity. The queerness of Christ's body reconfigures power, community, and love, offering a vision of sacred embodiment. Therefore, the holy Eucharist is not only a site of divine encounter but becomes a place of queer liberation.

If the sacrament is a symbol of Christ's union with the church, that union is between one whose body and gender are permeable and transcorporeal (Stuart 2007, 73). The body of Christ transcends singular definitions as it is a body that bleeds, breaks, transforms, and resurrects. Christ's body defies the logic of purity, hierarchy, and binary. In the sacramental encounter, we receive a body that queers our understanding of flesh and spirit, self and other, and divine and human. The union with Christ is a radical reimagining of love, kinship, and embodiment. It invites all bodies into the sacred space of becoming, of being made whole not through conformity but through communion.

The church is a community under a mandate to be queer. It is within the ecclesial body that queer theory finds its theological *telos*. Through baptism, the Christian is incorporated into the death and rising of Christ which is a radical reorientation that dismantles fixed identities (Stuart 2007, 75). In this mystery, the body of Christ becomes the site of transformation. Queer flesh is sacramental flesh that disrupts and reimagines. Sacramental flesh in queer flesh nudges the church itself toward deeper theological awakening where grace is experienced. In this sacramental vision, the body of Christ is not bound by binaries but is expansive, transformative, and queer. This is how the church experiences a communion of difference reconciled through love.

INDECENT THEOLOGY

Argentinian queer feminist theologian Marcella Althaus-Reid (2001) suggested an "indecent theology" to challenge traditional "decent" theologies that are heteronormative, misogynist, racist, and imperialist (2). She argued that all theologies are sexual because they are rooted in binary systems of gender and sexuality and are obsessed with sexual behaviors. Decent theologies are those with strict boundaries, especially around sexuality. Decent theologies impose constraints on sexuality and sexual expression and police sexual boundaries through punishment, expulsion, and even violence. Christianity and Christian theologies need to be liberated from decent theologies, especially their embrace of heterosexuality, according to Althaus-Reid. Theology's normative sexual ideology includes heteronormative beliefs about emotional and physical attractions, sexual prohibitions, marriage, the nuclear family, and women's submission. All of these work together to constrain human bodies, minds, and lives and reinforce unjust structures of heteronormativity.

By way of contrast to decent theology's assumption of heterosexuality, Althaus-Reid suggests indecent theologies. Indecent theologies are promiscuous—they love without boundaries. In indecent theologies, God is present and revealed in intimate acts, intimate human relationships, and loving exchanges.

Storytelling is a primary method of indecent theology because indecent stories problematize layers of oppression. They help us see and analyze the intersections. They also challenge the traditional order of decency by uncovering and undressing injustice. Althaus-Reid said that to disrupt norms of decency, indecency requires theological and sexual honesty.

Queer theologies are indecent because they interrupt theology as usual and unsettle sexual and theological complacencies that help maintain systems of injustice.

For example, Althaus-Reid argued that theology needs to liberate God from the heteronormative theologies that have closeted God. For her, God is not at the center but on the margins, in exile with exiled people like queer people (2004, 146). This God is among queers and is queer in God's challenge to oppressive norms and practices, including those of the church. Within the framework of indecency, Jesus then becomes the Unjust Messiah. Althaus-Reid noted that Jesus was trained in the tradition of messianism in which he had the law on his side and would keep the law as the righteous and fair one. But she continued, Jesus exceeded the constraints of this restrictive understanding of justice, stepping outside the bounds of traditional justice and accepted standards. Instead, Jesus opted for "unrestricted, open, larger relationships" (2001, 156). She said that as the Unjust Messiah, Jesus reflected the ongoing conflict between the tight, policed boundaries of the church and the larger justice that reclaims pleasure and inclusive love.

QUEERING THE BIBLE

For most queer folks, the Bible is a weapon that has been used to clobber them with five particular passages (Genesis 18:20-19:26; Leviticus 18:22 and 20:13; Romans 1:18-32; I Corinthians 6:9-10; I Timothy 1:9-10). Read out of social and linguistic context, these passages may seem to forbid diverse sexualities, and many Christians and churches have wielded them to do great harm to LGBTQI+ people. In actuality, these passages do not speak of diverse sexualities as we now understand them. Those understandings of sexual identity are very recent, only beginning in the late 19th and early 20th centuries. All biblical references are about certain kinds of same-sex acts. In biblical times, people would have had no concept of homosexuality/queer sexuality as an identity. Therefore, nowhere does the Bible actually speak about expressions of sexual identity.

Also, a strong emphasis on procreation is characteristic of the ancient Hebrew understanding of sexuality. In early Hebrew history, a small band of Semitic people was struggling to survive, and, therefore, reproduction of children was extremely important. Ancient Hebrews also believed that the whole of nascent life was in semen. Women were merely vessels for incubation. Thus, any ejaculation of semen that was nonprocreative was seen as a waste, a deliberate destruction of human life needed for the survival of the group.

Ancient Hebrew culture was also characterized by patriarchal understandings of men and women. Therefore, we see that the Hebrew Bible does not even mention sexual acts between women. Sexual acts between men, however, were viewed contemptuously because they placed one man in the role of a woman, a lesser human being. Ancient Hebrews also believed that each individual man in the group represented the whole, and so when one man behaved sexually like a woman he brought degradation and shame both on himself as an individual and on all men in the group. A common practice in the ancient Middle East during battle was the subjection of captured men to anal rape. This practice expressed complete domination and contempt because it compromised the dignity of the man who was used by another man like a woman.

Furthermore, the Bible does not record a single word spoken by Jesus about same-sex acts. While Jesus had a lot to say about loving neighbors and enemies and caring for the vulnerable, not once did he mention same-sex acts. Surely, if same-sex prohibitions were important, Jesus would have at least mentioned them.

By the time of the early church, Paul developed certain understandings of sex acts based on his background as a Jew living under the Roman Empire. Primarily, this understanding was shaped by patriarchal notions of hierarchy. For Paul, God was at the top of the hierarchy, followed by Christ, then man, then woman, then the rest of creation. Any challenge to this hierarchy for Paul was perceived as a challenge to the divinely created order. Because same-sex acts between men placed a man in a woman's role and because same-sex acts between women excluded men from sexual relations entirely, Paul saw these acts as outside the divinely ordained hierarchy of creation.

Genesis 18:20-19:26. In brief, the first passage, the story of Sodom, speaks not about sexuality but about inhospitality. The men of Sodom do not seek consensual relationships with the visitors; they threaten to rape them. For ancient Hebrews, hospitality was a primary value. To mistreat a guest was considered a grave affront. Furthermore, since the threat is against the angels who are God's representatives, the threatened violence is also a direct sin against God. Later references in the Hebrew Bible and in the gospel of Luke say nothing about same-sex behaviors. Only very late in the Christian Testament period did biblical writers give the story a sexual interpretation. The story condemns, not homosexuality, but the inhospitality shown to Lot's guests.

Leviticus 18:22 and 20:13. The two passages in Leviticus are from what is known as the Holiness Code. The Holiness Code is a section of Leviticus that focuses on behaviors ancient Hebrews were expected to do (or not do) as a sign of their unique relationship to God. These behaviors marked them as different from other people in the area and set apart by God. The overarching theme of the holiness code is religious defilement and idolatry. Canaanite religions centered fertility, and sex, including same-sex acts, as a part of religious ritual. Furthermore, worship of Canaanite fertility deities threatened the exclusive claims of the God of the ancient Hebrews. Another concern for ancient Hebrews was ceremonial uncleanness. Ceremonial purity was a way of showing their distinctiveness as a people set apart for God. Thus, avoiding things that were defined as "unclean" was an important part of carrying out ceremonial law. Rules around blood and semen were an important part of these laws, and ejaculation made men ceremonially unclean. Same-sex acts between men then made both men unclean, and such an act was considered a misuse of semen under ritual purity standards.

Furthermore, contemporary dependence on literal readings of these passages ignores the admonitions of other parts of the holiness code, such as not wearing mixed fiber clothing, not eating meat and milk together, not eating blood, or not having tattoos. Few Christians would suggest these commandments still hold.

Romans 1:18-32. A great deal of debate about the passage in Romans centers on Paul's appeal to what is "natural" as an argument against same-sex relationships. What is "natural" in any context usually depends on culture, convention, and social custom. For example, in I Corinthians 11:14-15, Paul argues that nature teaches that long hair is degrading to men.

In Greek and Roman cultures during Paul's lifetime, same-sex relationships were to some extent an accepted social custom. For Paul, same-sex acts were a violation of the laws of Jewish custom. The list of sins in this passage would have been a common list of "Gentile failings" during Paul's time and would have been quite familiar to Paul's readers. Same-sex acts were one more example of how Gentiles, as ceremoniously impure people, were different from Jews. Abstaining from such practices, as a way of setting themselves apart from others, could be a source of pride for Paul's audience.

Just as the social context for understanding the story of Sodom as a story about inhospitality is essential, so is understanding Paul's comments here within the social context of idolatry and lust in his time. The passage is not about people who identify as queer engaged in relationships but rather, in Paul's understanding, heterosexual people (although Paul would not have thought in terms of sexual identities at all) involved in sexual relationships that used people and were characterized by promiscuity. Most of the same-sex practices known to Paul would have involved adultery—married people having sex with other people. Greek men at the time often had a wife and a young man as a lover on the side. In fact, for adult men citizens of the time, sex was never about mutuality. It always involved someone considered subordinate—women, boys, foreigners, enslaved people. Sex was about social difference and power, and so Paul would only have seen sex acts between men as exploitative. He associated same-sex acts with insatiable lust and greed and considered them a "rich man's sport."

I Corinthians 6:9-10; I Timothy 1:9-10. Finally, the passages from the Epistles rely on ancient Greek words for which we have lost the original meanings. The Greek words in these passages translated to imply same-sex relationships are problematic. *Malakoi* in the King James Version is translated "effeminate," and *arsenokoitai* is translated "abusers of themselves with mankind." The Revised Standard Versions of 1946 and 1952 arbitrarily combined these words and translated them "homosexuals." The original language, however, makes no reference to sexual orientations or identities. The Greek words seem to single out specific kinds of sexual practices that were considered deplorable. The words may refer to male prostitution. Whatever the practices, however, these words suggest that what the author was condemning were exploitative sexual behaviors. Young enslaved boys were often forced into sexual servitude, some having been kidnapped expressly for that purpose. One scholar suggests I Timothy 1:10 could be rendered, "male prostitutes, males who lie with them, and slave dealers to procure them" (Scroggs 1983, 120).

By contrast, queer feminist interpreters look to larger themes in the biblical text to affirm queer lives. They point to the many passages elevating love above all. The Books of Acts, as well, demonstrates the movement of the gospel outward as barriers fall to people formerly excluded from good news. The Bible, then, becomes in its queer feminist reading, a text that can challenge oppression and empower liberation.

Queer readings of the text also move beyond simply using the tools of historical criticism to offer more culturally and linguistically informed readings. Queer readings bring queer lenses to the text to disrupt its heteronormative bias and to reimagine its interpretations with queer sexualities at the center. Queer feminist readings challenge fixed notions of identity, challenge dualisms, and integrate race, social class, ability, and age into queer feminist readings.

Hebrew Bible scholar Mona West (2006) offers a queer feminist reading of the story of Ruth. She suggests the first chapter of the story is one of coming out. In that time, women had only two ways to be valued—either as an unmarried virgin in her father's house or child-producing wife in her husband's house. Naomi, Ruth, and Orpah, then, are worthless and on the margins of society. Orpah leaves Naomi, but Ruth "comes out," declaring her true feelings for Naomi. *Davka* (clinging) is the same word used in Genesis 2:24. ("Therefore a man leaves his father and his mother and clings to his wife.") Ruth's words declare their refusal to accept the status quo that limits and defines them as worthless based on their marital status and reproductive ability.

When they return to Bethlehem, they struggle to survive. Naomi realizes they need a longer-term strategy, and so she works within the framework of existing kinship laws to find a way for her, Ruth, and Boaz to form their own family. Ruth and Boaz have a son, and the women of the town say, "A son has been born to Naomi." In this queer feminist reading of Ruth, we see an affirmation of diverse kinds of families and non-normative relationships that challenge traditional heteronormative nuclear families.

RADICAL LOVE

Queer theologian Patrick Cheng sees queer theology, in its essence, as radical love, which he defines as "a love that is so extreme that it dissolved existing boundaries" (2011, 44). For Cheng, God's radical love dissolves boundaries between the Divine and human, the powerful and the weak, and knowing and unknowing. In fact, for Cheng, God is radical love itself. He adds that, as such, God "functions in the same way as LGBTQI+ people with respect to radical love. To the extent that LGBTQI+ people break down boundaries of sexuality and gender in our relationships, both God and LGBTQI+ people send forth a radical love that breaks down fixed categories and boundaries (51)." Cheng queers the traditional formulation of the Trinity by explaining that God sends forth radical love; that Jesus recovers the radical love that was lost by humans; and that the Holy Spirits shows how we return to radical love 139).

TRANS THEOLOGIES

Trans theologies are rooted in the deep truths of God's creation of diversity and God's love for all of creation. Despite conservative arguments that sex and gender are binary, science demonstrates that that's simply not true. All across nature, sex is more complicated and more diverse.

Transgender people have existed in all cultures across the world throughout human history, often appearing as a "third sex" in ancient artifacts. Neolithic and Bronze Age drawings depict humans with both male and female physical characteristics. A third-century BCE burial site in Prague contained a physically male body in clothes typically worn by women of the time. Writers across the centuries, dating back as far as the fourth century BCE, have recorded instances of third gender or transgender people.

Genesis 1 tells us that in the beginning God created humans in God's image, male and female. Rather than suggesting binary sex, that passage tells us that God is all genders, that the gender continuum resides in the being of God. God is transgender. God crosses gender, is all genders, and humans are made in God's image as many-gendered people.

Rabbi Mark Sameth (2016) writes about the highly elastic nature of gender in Hebrew Bible times: "In Genesis 3:12, Eve is referred to as "he." In Genesis 9:21, after the flood, Noah repairs to "her" tent. Genesis 24:16 refers to Rebecca as a "young man." And Genesis 1:27 refers to Adam as 'them.'" The rabbi continues:

> Why would the Bible do this? These aren't typos. In the ancient world, well-expressed gender fluidity was the mark of a civilized person. Such a person was considered more '"godlike.' In Ancient Mesopotamia and Egypt, the gods were thought of as gender-fluid, and human beings were considered reflections of the gods.
>
> The Israelites took the transgender trope from their surrounding cultures and wove it into their own sacred scripture. The four-Hebrew-letter name of God, which scholars refer to as the Tetragrammaton, YHWH, was probably not pronounced 'Jehovah' or 'Yahweh,' as some have guessed. The Israelite priests would have read the letters in reverse as Hu/Hi—in other words, the hidden name of God was Hebrew for 'He/She.' Counter to everything we grew up believing, the God of Israel—the God of the three monotheistic, Abrahamic religions to which fully half the people on the planet today belong—was understood by its earliest worshipers to be a dual-gendered deity.

If we continue to look for these images of trans—across, crossing over—in the Bible, we see that the idea of trans is central to Christian understandings of faith. Not only does God cross genders, but the Israelites cross the Red Sea on dry land, they cross over the Jordan River into the Promised Land, Jesus crosses over the Sea of Galilee; in incarnation God crosses over from deity into humanity, the gospel of John says we have crossed over from death to life, and Jesus himself crosses over from death into resurrection. Christians still use this metaphor of crossing over to show transformation. They sing, "I'm just a-going over Jordan. I'm just a-going over home." "I won't have to cross Jordan alone." "My home is over Jordan."

Trans theologies challenge binaries and boundaries and open up space for ambiguity, uncertainty, and change. Trans theologies are transgressive. They resist, challenge, and confront traditional theologies that constrain and contain human possibilities. Minister and theologian B. K. Hipsher explains, for example, that trans theologies compel us to imagine God "in the ever-changing, shifting, diverse, and multiple transgender realities that human beings embody" and adds that a trans God "transgresses all of our ideas about who and what God is and can be" (2006, 99).

Trans feminist theologian Virginia Ramey Mollenkott suggests that trans theologies have an important role to play within Christianity. She says that the very presence of trans people can help overcome the stereotypes of gender that alienate men from their own bodies and oppress women all over the world (2006, 49). Trans people make visible the continuum of gender and thus the unity of all genders. All diversities, she argues, "point toward one great Spirit who chose to incarnate in millions of different forms" (57).

Trans feminist theologies also remind us that bodies matter in our theologizing. Alex Clare-Young explains that trans people are "literally fleshing out trans-related theology" (2024, 16). Trans theologies are rooted in trans bodies and trans meaning. Rather than looking for unifying theories or theologies, trans theologies reject essentialist notions of gender and sexuality and demand fragmentation, a recognition and valuing of the differences of each individual person. Trans theologies, then, are not representative of a group but rather emerge from unique experiences of individuals who each have something to contribute to the theological conversation. As a form of body theology, trans theologies cannot be limited by the assumption of normative bodies, and this must be inclusive of disabled bodies as well as trans bodies. The full range of body diversity must be part of trans theologizing.

HETEROSEXUAL DISSENTERS

Queer feminist theologies offer the possibility for heterosexual people to engage in non-heteronormative theology as well. In so doing, they can help Christianity come out of the closet and be more authentic in God's love and justice. Queer theologian Susannah Cornwall is herself heterosexual, cis-gender, and married to a cis-gender, heterosexual man. Still, she has written extensively in queer theologies and has pioneered intersex theologies. She acknowledges debates about whether or not non-queer people can do queer theology. She explains, "I do not claim a right to speak on behalf of others; rather, I seek to speak *with* them, reflecting on how queer theology implicates and interrogates all Christians, whatever their sex, sexuality and gender identity" (2011, 5). For her work in intersex theology, *Sex and Uncertainty in the Body of Christ*, Cornwall interviewed intersex people who expressed their satisfaction with their bodies as God intended. For Cornwall, intersex bodies challenge the privilege of "clearly-sexed, heteronormative configurations of sexes, sexualities, and gender to the exclusion of people whose bodies or identities do not 'fit'. This reflects back into all manner of theological assertion about the meaning and significance of gender: it becomes far more difficult to unproblematically assert that women should not be ordained, or be made bishops, if we can no longer be quite so certain of what a woman actually is" (2014, 16–17).

As a heterosexual dissenter, Cornwall turns a queer gaze on, for example, institutions that privilege heterosexuality, like marriage, and offers critique and challenge. She proposes an "un/familiar theology" that appraises the current state of theologies of marriage, family, and reproduction transposed against the complex lived realities of human experience that are, in many ways, "unfamiliar" to Christian tradition. She argues that the changes in same-sex marriage and parenting by same-sex couples and single people alter traditional understandings of marriage, family, and parenting, but these are not departures to be mourned but shifts to be critically engaged (2017, 2). Christians, she reminds, do not own marriage, and God did not invent marriage; humans did, and so they can reinvent it (2017, 46).

By dissenting from the norms and privileges of heterosexuality, Cornwall offers a model for heterosexuals to participate in non-normative queer theologies that disrupt heteronormativity and make space for diverse people and experiences. Her work demonstrates the breadth and depth of possibilities for queer theologies to contest traditional theologies, especially their privileging of heterosexuality and the gender binary. By centering the complex and complicated bodies and lives of queer, trans, and intersex people, queer theologies assert the right of queer, trans, and intersex people to exist and to be diverse expressions of God's image and insist on the liberatory power of queerness as theological method.

NOTE

1. For more detail on queer theologies, see *Queer Theologies: The Basics*, another book in Routledge's The Basics Series, authored by Chris Greenough.

BIBLIOGRAPHY

Althaus-Reid, Marcella. 2001. *Indecent Theology: Theological Perspectives in Sex, Gender, and Politics*. Routledge.

Althaus-Reid, Marcella. 2004. *From Feminist to Indecent Theology*. SCM Press.

Bong, Sharon. 2007. "Queer Revisions of Christianity," p. 234–249. In *Body and Sexuality Theological-Pastoral Perspectives of Women in Asia*, Eds. A. M. Brazal & A. L. Si.

Cheng, Patrick. 2011. *Radical Love: Introduction to Queer Theology*. Seabury Books.

Clare-Young, Alex. 2024. "Introduction," p. 7–33. In *Trans Formations: Grounding Theology in Trans and Non-Binary Lives*, Ed. Alex Clare-Young.

Contreras, M. A. 2024. "Inhabiting Adamancy: Contributions Toward a Queer Feminist Theology." *Feminist Theology*, 32 (3): 270–282. https://doi-org.proxy.earlham.edu/10.1177/09667350241233570 (Original work published 2024).

Cornwall, Susannah. 2011. *Controversies in Queer Theology*. SCM.

Cornwall, Susannah. 2014. *Sex and Uncertainty in the Body of Christ*. Routledge.

Cornwall, Susannah. 2017. *Un/familiar Theology: Reconceiving Sex, Reproduction and Generativity*. Bloomsbury Academic.

Hipsher, B. K. 2006. "'God Is a Many-Gendered Thing' An Apophatic Journey to Pastoral Diversity," p. 92–104. In *Trans/Formations*, Eds. Althaus-Reid Marcella & Lisa Isherwood.

Lightsey, Pamela. 2015. *Our Lives Matter: A Womanist Queer Theology*. Wipf and Stock.

Mollenkott, Virginia Ramey. 2006. "We Come Bearing Gifts: Seven Lessons Religious Congregations Can Learn from Transpeople," p. 46–58. In *Trans/Formations*, Eds. Marcella Althaus-Reid and Lisa Isherwood. SCM.

Sameth, Mark. 2016. "Is God Transgender?" *New York Times*, https://www.nytimes.com/2016/08/13/opinion/is-god-transgender.html. Accessed March 7, 2025.

Scroggs, Robin. 1983. *The New Testament and Homosexuality*. Fortress Press.

Stuart, Elizabeth. 2007. "Sacramental Flesh," p. 65–75. In *Queer Theology: Rethinking the Western Body*, Ed. Gerard Loughlin. Blackwell Publishing.

West, Mona. 2006. "Ruth," p. 190–194. In *The Queer Bible Commentary*, Eds. Deryn Guest, Robert E. Goss, Mona West & Thomas Bohace. SCM Press.

FEMINIST DISABILITY THEOLOGIES

While feminist theologies have offered a necessary corrective to patriarchal theology's dismissal or demonization of the body, their emphasis on the body has, at times, contributed to ableism by not recognizing the different perspectives disabled bodies bring to the theological conversation. Feminist disability theologies challenge the able-bodied assumptions of many feminist theologies and construct theologies grounded in diverse disabled bodies that speak to the complications of bodies within theologies. In many theologies, feminist or otherwise, disabled bodies are often invisible; yet disability is a central human experience. Many of us experience severe and lifelong disabilities; all of us experience disability at some point in our lives, even if it is temporary. Yet most feminist theologies have assumed a fully able body and therefore have not explored the intersections of disability with sexism. Queer theologies have been somewhat more likely to engage disabled bodies because, in many ways, a disabled body is inherently queer in an able-bodied world.

Within patriarchy's dualistic framework of men or women/mind or body, the identification of women with the body proved a key justification for discrimination against women. As bodies, women were situated as less like God/Spirit than men. Feminist theology's embrace of the body makes sense as a response to the denigration of women's bodies in patriarchy. Yet, when we center disability in our thinking, we recognize that ableism and sexism intersect in important ways for theological thinking. Disabled bodies are feminized within

DOI: 10.4324/9781032643939-10

patriarchy. They are viewed as weak, passive, dependent, damaged, needy, less than—like women. Disabled bodies, like female bodies, force us to reckon with questions of materiality, flesh, blood and guts, and pain. Disabled bodies, like female bodies, are positioned as inherently defective within patriarchy, as something to be fixed or cured or accommodated. Similarly, trans bodies are problematized and devalued as flawed, if not sinful.

Feminists are actively working to dismantle patriarchal dualism, which historically privileged the masculine mind or spirit over the feminine body or physicality. As part of this effort, they are reclaiming the concept of disability and its material realities, challenging its past treatment as part of a cultural strategy rooted in dualistic thinking (Betcher 2010, 107). Dualism has consistently favored and elevated men over women, shaping the field of disability studies in gendered ways.

Too often, disability is treated as an "and" statement, added on after discussions of race, gender, class, and sexuality, as if it were a separate, secondary concern. This framing reduces disability to an addendum rather than recognizing it as an integral part of broader social justice conversations. Scholars who focus on disability are frequently seen as dealing with "special" interests, with the assumption that they must have a personal connection to the subject. Such assumptions not only flatten the complexity of disability but also obscure its embodied realities, relegating it to a marginalized space, both conceptually and socially (Creamer 2010, 124). Disability should not be confined to closed or specialized spaces of discussion, it belongs in open, inclusive conversations alongside other critical areas of research. It deserves the same level of attention, rigor, and importance as topics like race, gender, class, and sexuality.

We must also confront the issue of sexism within the disability movement and disability studies The movement's agenda has often been shaped by gendered assumptions, and it's crucial that we begin to question and challenge this dynamic. Greater investment is needed in research that centers disability within the feminist movement, bringing it into the mainstream rather than leaving it at the margins. Building supportive alliances between women with and without disabilities is essential, as is working collectively toward the empowerment of women with disabilities (Yong 2007, 129). The absence of this critical work makes it increasingly urgent to pursue so that the fight for liberation includes all women, not just those who are able-bodied.

DISABILITY AND ABLEISM

Laws and dictionaries typically define disability as a physical or mental impairment that substantially limits a person's ability to engage in typical life activities. Physical disabilities include mobility impairment, chronic diseases, blindness and vision impairment, and deafness and hearing impairment. Cognitive or mental disabilities include learning disabilities, addictions, developmental difficulties, autism, and emotional/behavioral disorders. Disabilities can also be short-term and temporary or long-term, apparent and non-apparent, congenital and acquired, painful and not painful.

The dominant paradigms of disability identify disability with the body. The medical model insists that disability is a disease that is curable and/or treatable. The charity model situates disability as a tragedy or misfortune to be addressed through generous giving. The "supercrip" model argues that disability is a challenge to be overcome, and the moral model turns disability into a sign of moral weakness or failing.

In contrast, the social model of disability locates the problem, not in individual bodies, but in social institutions and structures created by and for able-bodied persons in such a way that they create disabling effects. At its best, the social model recognizes the complex interaction between bodies and institutions and strives to challenge institutions to remove as many disabling barriers as possible and create as many supportive structures as they can. For example, if a wheelchair user encounters a multi-storied building that does not have a ramp, elevator, wide hallways, wide bathroom stalls with grab bars, then the building itself prevents the wheelchair user from entering or being able to maneuver in the building.

In this case, the problem is not the body's impairment but the building's obstruction. As long as the wheelchair user can get into the building and use it with ease, they are not disabled in relation to using the building. They are only disabled in using the building if the building itself prevents them from being able to use it. At the same time, we must recognize that for the wheelchair user their physical impairment is an important aspect of who they are and may be an individual problem for them. Disability, in the social model, does not have to be an inevitable consequence of impairment; rather it most often comes as a result of prejudice, discrimination, and lack of accommodations.

Ableism is a form of discrimination against people with physical, mental, or developmental disabilities. It is characterized by beliefs that these people need to be fixed or cured, that they cannot function fully in society, and that their disability makes them of less value to society if not an outright burden on society. Ableism depends on stereotypes, institutions, and violence to maintain able-bodied dominance and subjugate people with impairments. Stereotypes, such as "cripple," "mental patient," and "druggie" send clear messages about how dominant society views disabilities and serve to dehumanize and other people who have impairments. Institutions often discriminate against and mistreat people with impairments. For example, workplaces may fight to deny accommodations, or medical providers may judge and put down people for their size. Media often show people with disabilities in ways that, though often well-intended, serve to other them. For example, many images depict people with disabilities as wonderous overcomers of hardship. That suggests that people who do not overcome are somehow responsible for their own situation. People with impairments may experience violence in a number of ways, from constraints on movement to medication against their will to incarceration to beatings and sexual assault. We know, for example, that people with cognitive impairments are more susceptible to sexual violence than people without. These forms of violence maintain able-bodied dominance and further subjugate people with disabilities.

Feminist disability theorists emphasize the link between the politics of appearance and the medicalization of marginalized women's bodies. They argue that societal standards around appearance and health function as tools of discipline, reinforcing systems of power that label certain bodies, especially those of women and people with disabilities, as "abnormal." The female body, in particular, has been subjected to medical scrutiny and regulation, framed as something inherently in need of control or correction. Historically, both women and disabled individuals have been perceived through a medicalized lens that casts them as biologically deficient. This framing contributes to the gendering of sickness as feminine, further entrenching the harmful stereotype of women as the weaker sex. The intersection of gender and disability reveals how oppression is sustained through both medical and social narratives, calling for a critical reevaluation of the norms that define health, normalcy, and strength (Ahlvik-Harju 2016, 223). When the medical field perpetuates these negative narratives about women, it deepens their oppression and marginalization. It is essential to rethink how we understand women and their bodies in ways that do not contribute to their continued subjugation.

Society often pathologizes women's bodies, reinforcing stereotypes of weakness or abnormality, especially for those who fall outside societal norms. To address these concerns and harms, we need to rethink how women and their bodies are understood within medical and societal contexts. This requires moving away from views that reduce women to their biological "deficits" and instead embracing holistic perspectives that honor women's complexity and agency. There must be a shift toward more inclusive, compassionate approaches that empower women, recognizing their strength, autonomy, and diverse experiences. By advocating for more equitable and respectful perspectives and understanding, we can work toward dismantling the oppressive structures that persist within both the medical field and society at large.

The consequences of how society views women's bodies and disabled bodies are profound and deeply troubling. One of the most devastating outcomes is that these bodies become targets for elimination and death. People with disabilities, those who are disfigured, queer individuals, and people of color have historically been subjected to infanticide, selective abortion, eugenics programs, assisted suicide, and invasive surgical procedures aimed at "fixing" or harming their bodies. Beyond these practices, women are also vulnerable to violent crimes, abuse, and neglect. These realities are legitimized by dominant systems of representation that shape our perceptions and influence the material world. Recognizing these injustices is one of the first critical steps toward developing a more just and compassionate understanding of bodies—a shift that challenges harmful ideologies and works toward dismantling the systems that perpetuate violence and discrimination (Ahlvik-Harju 2016, 223). Becoming aware of these injustices is one of the crucial first steps toward fostering a more just and inclusive understanding of bodies.

We must actively resist the ghettoization of disability and instead center critical reflection on ableism as a fundamental feminist concern. Feminists have a responsibility to challenge the privatization of disability—the tendency to treat it as an individual issue rather than a systemic one. Despite the work of disability theorists in emphasizing that disability is socially constructed and enacted, it is still widely perceived as a personal pathology. This individualizing framework obscures the broader dynamics of stigma, shame, and fear that sustain a body politic obsessed with physical independence, productivity, and perfection. As a result, society pressures us to hide or "fix" bodily differences, teaching us to fear weakness, deny vulnerability, imagine ourselves as invincible, and ultimately reject those who visibly remind us of our own limitations. Feminist and disability theologians alike must recognize the body as a vital site of shared struggle and solidarity—one that calls us into deeper reflection on justice, dignity, and human interconnectedness (Belser 2023, 130). We must continue to examine the dynamics of our flesh and bodies, and how societal politics pressure us into harmful ways of viewing and treating bodies that deviate from normative standards. These forces confine us, shaping our perceptions through fear, shame, and exclusion. To move toward justice, we must liberate ourselves from these constraints and embrace a theology that affirms and uplifts all bodies, especially disabled bodies. Such a theology recognizes the sacredness of difference, challenges systems of devaluation, and calls us into a more inclusive and compassionate understanding of embodiment.

OTHERING OF BODIES

Feminist theory has often described difference in terms of othering. Women with disabilities have been othered to men and also to non-disabled women to the point that, in many ways, women with disabilities are not seen as women in society at all. Othering entails two processes. First is grouping people together as the objects of our experience instead of regarding them as subjects of experience with whom we might identify. The second is viewing them as symbols for something we fear. The symbolic meanings of a person, such as race, gender, or sexual identity may make them the other. For example, cultural assumptions about disability that encompass weakness, dependency, and helplessness clash with cultural assumptions of masculinity. However, this assumption overlaps with the cultural assumptions of femininity so that a disabled man is perceived as a "wounded male," and therefore feminized, while a disabled woman still fulfills cultural expectations, although she is often either desexualized or fetishized. These perceptions illustrate how disability and illness are gendered feminine (Ahlvik-Harju 2016, 226).

The otherness of disabled women is maintained by dominant culture through stereotypes, invisibility, and barriers. The normalcy of broken bodies is not accepted, as evident in commercials, pictures, books, and images. People with disabilities are rarely included in descriptions and images of ordinary life. Furthermore, the daily struggles, thoughts, and feelings of people with disabilities are oftentimes excluded from any shared cultural understanding of human experience. As people with disabilities are made invisible, the gap between disabled and able-bodied people gets wider (Ahlvik-Harju 2016, 227). Thus, a femininst theology disability needs to tackle the othering and objectifying of disabled women's bodies and make the case for embracing them as full bodies within culture and society. They need to be made visible, and their issues, concerns and significance also needs to be raised and elevated.

FEMINIST DISABILITY THEOLOGY

While feminist thinkers early recognized the centrality of embodiment for women's liberation, they often overlooked or ignored disabled and trans bodies. Too often, feminists assumed fully able bodies and accepted the logic of fit and whole bodies as normative. Feminist disability thinkers challenged these ideas and encouraged other feminists to reclaim all bodies as the subject of feminist embodiment. Sharon V. Betcher suggests that disability refers us to a "deep anxiety inherent in humanism's relation to the flesh—a fear of being 'humiliated' (from the same Latin root as 'humus' or Earth) by life. When bodies are labeled disabled, society marks out and makes these refused others carry the dread fear of the precarious vulnerability of flesh" (2010, 110). In other words, women, people with disabilities, people of color, and LGBTQI+ people have all been taught to loathe their own flesh, surveil it, and control it.

Betcher argues that feminist and disability theologies should work together to rethink flesh (113). For example, rethinking discourses on pain should be a key conversation for feminist disability theologies. Traditionally, theologies have constructed pain as a result of sin or as a burden to be transcended. What might this conversation become if people who live in chronic pain were at the center, or if we say pain is a moral necessity (Holler 2002, 78)? What might be the value of pain? Certainly, theology has also served as a site for discrimination and violence against people with disabilities. Disabilities have been framed as punishment for sin or as God's will. As an institution, the church has often excluded people with disabilities through its lack of accommodations, or it has offered judgment, as in the cases of HIV/AIDS and addictions. Glossing over the realities of Jesus' suffering in favor of rushing to the resurrection is yet another way the church avoids dealing with the realities of pain and suffering, especially for those who live with physical, mental, and developmental impairments.

Feminist disability theologies challenge the dominance of ableism and the church's role as an ableist institution. The church has often engaged in the very stereotypes and violence that perpetuate ableism, and feminist disability theologies offer correctives to this historical and contemporary practice of the church. For example, often the church uses the metaphors of deafness and blindness to signify sinfulness or refusal to heed God's direction. How often have we sung, "I once was lost but now am found, was blind but now I see" as part of our worship services? Too often, church buildings or services are inaccessible to people with disabilities, and, in some Christian traditions, adherents suggest that healing would come if only people had enough faith. Churches, too, can appear magnanimous with acts of charity toward people with disabilities, while, in reality, they disempower them through biases in language, structures, and theology.

Feminist disability theologies challenge us to ask hard questions about bodies. For example, most able-bodied people assume all people with disabilities want to be cured or fixed. We are not able to see the possibilities of disabilities as gifts that can bring unique and transformative insights to our theological conversations. On the other hand, assumptions of able-bodiedness prevent us from theologically exploring issues like chronic pain, infertility, terminal illness, end-stage cancer, and physician assisted-suicide. Feminist disability theologies invite us to hear the diverse voices of people living with disabilities and to learn from them what their experiences have to say to theological questions. They help us examine and resist the "disabling effects of patriarchy" that we experience at the intersections of sexism, ableism, racism, classism, ageism, and heterosexism (Freeman 2002, 6).

A woman with a disability perceives and imagines God through the lens of her lived experiences. Her encounters with brokenness, marginalization, and subordination profoundly shape her metaphors and understanding of the divine and provide perspectives that can enrich theological conversations for all people. Feminist disability theologies must therefore resist the patriarchal politics of division that upholds the ability/disability divide. Dividing women along these lines undermines the broader struggle against sexist oppression and weakens the sense of communal responsibility rooted in interconnectedness and shared humanity. This false dichotomy creates unnecessary barriers between bodies and must be dismantled. Instead, feminist disability theologies should pursue solidarity and harmony, recognizing that all women, regardless of ability, class, race, or sexuality, face discrimination rooted in gender. While attentive to differences, the shared experience of subordination can unite, rather than divide, women in the fight for justice (Chisale 2020, 2). The harmful binaries that set women against one another—often along lines of ability, identity, and experience—damage all women. To move forward, we must listen to each other's stories and reject the false dichotomy that positions disability as a dividing line among women. Women of all identities, bodies, classes, and ethnicities must come together to dismantle the patriarchal systems that thrive on division. Moreover, we must also confront other forms of oppression—racism, ableism, classism, heterosexism—that intersect with patriarchy. This is no longer an "us versus them" defined by ability or body. The path to justice demands solidarity. We must stand with one another, fight alongside one another, and recognize that no one wins this struggle alone. Only together can we challenge and overcome the structures that seek to keep us apart.

We desperately need different ways of viewing our bodies and disabled bodies that do not undermine one's humanity. We need to view people with disabled bodies as part of the kin-dom of God, as they provide deep insights into who we are as human beings and who God is. Disabled bodies remind us of our vulnerability and how we, as human beings, need to practice empathy and compassion. Disabled bodies also confront us with the possibility of our own pain and the need to handle our pain (Ahlvik-Harju 2016, 225). In particular, feminist disability theologies must remind us that our bodies are not a curse because of sin but a blessing that allows all people to experience through their senses the beauty, creativity, and love of God.

THEOLOGY OF A DISABLED GOD

Nancy Eiesland (1994) noted that, within the church as a whole, people with disabilities were, at best, tolerated, if not outright excluded (82–86). She faulted traditional theologies that devalued people with disabilities and acted paternalistically toward them. Instead, she suggested, the church needed theologies of liberation that centered experiences of disability as normal parts of life rather than as problems to be solved or accommodated. These differences in bodies, she argued, could provide different viewpoints from which to imagine God for all people.

Because the church has traditionally viewed God as perfect, it has viewed disabilities as imperfections, if not results of sin. For the church, to be like God is to be perfect, not only in behavior, but also in body and mind. Disabilities, then, are barriers to be overcome in the present and deficiencies to be banished in an eternal world to come. Process theology critiques the notion of God as perfect, immutable, and stagnant. Rather, process theology suggests God is dynamic, changing, and immanent. This theology frees us from the expectations of perfection, including bodily perfection and eliminates the dichotomy between abled and disabled bodies.

Eisland suggests that since Jesus' wounds remain post-resurrection, the resurrected Christ becomes a symbol of the disabled God. Jewish scholar Julia Watts Belser describes the joy she felt at reading a passage in Ezekiel 1 that describes God on wheels. Belser, herself a wheelchair user, explains that she experiences freedom and power in using her wheelchair, and she suggests that, if God has wheels, God, too, knows wheelchair users' experiences of joy and frustration. Heike Peckruhn (2024) adds, "Without imagining and speaking of a disabled God, a God who shares and knows all disability experiences intimately, we cannot begin to investigate the social and theological structures that impede God's full presence in this world."

Building on Eisland's work and drawing on Bruce McCormack's Barthian theology of the trinity, Lisa D. Powell (2023) suggests that as the eternal second person of the Trinity Jesus means that God has always been broken. Powell notes that often theologians have used the language of brokenness and suffering to subjugate women and other minoritized people. She argues instead of passivity, we can understand Jesus' brokenness and suffering as instances of receptivity which is engaged and active. Instead of the language of obedience to describe Jesus' relationship to God, she suggests the language of "call and response." The risk of incarnation, she explains, was that God called, not forced, Jesus to obedience. God, then, becomes vulnerable to human agency, and human actions affect God who is not "wholly other."

FEMINIST ETHICS OF CARE AND INTERDEPENDENCE

At the core of feminist ethics are the concepts of care and interdependence. Rather than flowing one way as pity or charity, feminist care is mutual and requires interdependence in which all parties bring value to relationships. Feminist disability ethics challenge the tendency of the church to avoid deep theological analysis of disability and action alongside people with disabilities. Theologically, they challenge "disability as a marvelous plot device, to show God's power" (Freeman 2002, 80), instead embracing people with disabilities as equal co-creators in liberatory theologies. Freeman adds, "The more we make vulnerable, suffering bodies visible the more we will face up to our own deterioration. and society's lack of provision for the disabled and the aged and the lack of discourse about illnesses" (84).

Feminist theologian Lisa Isherwood suggests the disabled Christ "highlights the necessity for mutuality and interdependence" (2002, 100). She says that we are offered a Christ who needs care and mutuality. The disabled Christ also challenges patriarchal myths of independence and individualism and instead underscores our human need for healthy, mutual, and sustaining relationships. This Christ affirms vulnerability not as weakness but as a sacred space where grace, community, and healing can emerge. Christ is scarred and wounded but also experiences resurrection. This invites us to a sense of mutual care and affirmation.

Feminist theology has long critiqued hierarchical power structures that devalue bodies marked as "other," while disability theology centers and focuses on the lived experiences of those whose bodies resist normative standards. This provides theological lenses to affirm that all bodies, able, disabled, broken, disfigured, or maimed, carry divine worth. Therefore, liberation is found not in isolation or perfection but in community, connection, and shared struggle. The disabled Christ then becomes a necessary radical symbol of hope and solidarity—one who embraces the realities of pain and marginalization yet also redeems them through love and relational wholeness. This is the Christ that feminist disability theologies assert can transform lives and communities to welcome diversity into the body of Christ.

According to Dora Inés Munévar, an ethic of care "seeks socio-political, legal, economic, familial, and interpersonal transformation in relational and reciprocal terms" (2021, 219). A feminist ethic of care challenges heteropatriarchal notions of independence and autonomy and normative images of individualism and self-centeredness. In relation to disability, feminist ethics of care and interdependence reject notions of care as confinement, imposition, disregard, and dependence that are normally experienced in social institutions tasked with supporting people with disabilities, that often see people with disabilities as passive subjects. In these instances, "care" itself is oppressive. Instead, disability activists demand "assistance" rather than care as traditionally defined and practiced.

Feminist disability ethics, by contrast, recognize that people with disabilities are active participants in relationships of caring and are capable of a great degree of self-determination and advocacy. Autonomy of people with disabilities is respected and valued, and recognition of diversity is central. In particular, feminist disability ethics pay attention to the intersections of gender, race, and other forms of social difference with disability to contest the ways ableism is also a practice of racism, heteropatriarchy, and capitalism. Feminist philosopher Eva Feder Kittay argues that care, which is interpersonal, and justice, which is institutional, are not opposite or unrelated. Rather, she argues that making an ethics of care central to a theory of justice would require reconciling rights with the need to honor responsibilities toward people who rely on us and the task of meeting individual needs with the policies and practices of institutions that center a generalized other, resulting in rules that overlook the specific needs of individual people (Gesser and Fietz 2021).

Feminist disability ethics challenge the church to rethink its approach to people with disabilities. Rather than imagining care as a task church members do for people with disabilities, the church must see care as a mutual task carried out by all in the church through interdependent relationships. Churches can begin by empowering people with disabilities to make their own decisions about their place in the church. They can tell the church what they need from the congregation. They can also offer their gifts to the congregation. The church should be a place for radical belonging for all people, and people with disabilities must be equal participants in the creation of the church.

BIBLIOGRAPHY

Ahlvik-Harju, Carolin. 2016. "Disturbing Bodies – Reimagining Comforting Narratives of Embodiment Through Feminist Disability Studies." *Scandinavian Journal of Disability Research*, 18 (3): 222–233.

Belser, Julia Watts. 2010. "Returning to Flesh: A Jewish Reflection on Feminist Disability, Theology." *Journal of Feminist Studies in Religion*, 26 (2): 127–132.

Belser, Julia Watts. 2023. *Loving Our Own Bones: Disability Wisdom and the Spiritual Subversiveness of Knowing Ourselves Whole*. Beacon Press.

Betcher, Sharon V. 2010. "Becoming Flesh of My Flesh: Feminist and Disability Theologies on the Edge of Posthumanist Discourse." *Journal of Feminist Studies in Religion*, 26 (2): 107–118.

Chisale, Sinenhlanhla Sithulisiwe. 2020. "The Purity Myth: A Feminist Disability Theology of Women's Sexuality and Implications for Pastoral Care." *Scriptura*, 119 (1): 1–11.

Creamer, Deborah Beth. 2010. "Embracing Limits, Queering Embodiment: Creating/Creative Possibilities for Disability Theology." *Journal of Feminist Studies in Religion*, 26 (2): 124.

Eiesland, Nancy L. 1994. *The Disabled God: Toward a Liberatory Theology of Disability.* Abingdon Press.

Freeman, Doreen. 2002. "A Feminist Theology of Disability." *Feminist Theology*, 10 (29): 71–85.

Gesser, Marivete and Helena Fietz. 2021. "Ethics of Care and the Experience of Disability: An Interview with Eva Feder Kittay." *Revista Estudos Feministas*, 29 (2). https://doi.org/10.1590/1806-9584-2021v29n264987

Holler, Linda. 2002. *Erotic Morality: The Role of Touch in Moral Agency.* Rutgers University Press

Isherwood, Lisa. 2002. *Introducing Feminist Christologies.* The Pilgrim Press.

Munévar M., Dora Inés. 2021. "Dialogues Between (Feminist) Studies of Care and (Critical) Disability Studies to Rethink Emerging Activisms," In *Care and Care Workers. Latin American Societies*, Eds. Nadya Araujo Guimarães & Helena Hirata. Springer. https://doi.org/10.1007/978-3-030-51693-2_13

Peckruhn, Heike. 2024. "A Disabled God: Disabilities as Divine Possibilities." *Vision: A Journal for Church and Theology*, 25 (2).

Powell, Lisa D. 2023. *The Disabled God Revisited: Trinity, Christology, and Liberation.* T & T Clark.

Yong, Amos. 2007. *Theology and Down Syndrome: Reimagining Disability in Late Modernity.* Baylor University Press.

EPILOGUE

Feminist Theologies: A Path Toward Liberation and Justice

Feminist theologies matter not just for women but for all people seeking justice, equity, and liberation. They offer a vital lens through which we can examine history, culture, and religion. They also help confront present realities and envision a more inclusive and just future. Feminist theologies are not a monolithic concept, as feminist theologies are intersectional, dynamic, experiential, and contextual. Feminist theologies acknowledge that women's experiences are shaped by many factors such as race, sexuality, disability, ethnicity, culture, location, language, age, ableism, economics, and more. That is why feminist theologies continue to evolve: because the lived experiences of women in different contexts are diverse, rich, and ever-changing. As feminist theologies continue to change, newer ways and methods of doing theology will continue to emerge to address the various concerns that will arise from different contexts and experiences.

This book, *Feminist Theology: The Basics*, explores different feminist theologies that serve as tools and methods for understanding the complex ways oppressions operate around the globe and also within their ethnic communities or communities to which they belong. Whether it's racism, ableism, climate injustice, or economic inequality, feminist theologies help us uncover the deep intersections that marginalize women in distinct and devastating ways and offer paths toward activism, change, and transformation to a more socially just and environmentally responsible world.

The goal of doing feminist theology is to dismantle patriarchy (along with white supremacy, heterosexism, wealth inequality, ableism, ageism, and all other forms of oppression), not only within the church, but across every part of life. Each theological perspective in the book addresses how power structures impact women and how people can seek pathways toward liberation, empowerment, and flourishing. These perspectives also call attention to the ways Christianity and theology have influenced gender dynamics, particularly through how the Bible has been written, interpreted, and taught.

For centuries, the Bible has been understood primarily through patriarchal eyes, written mostly by men, for men, in patriarchal contexts. Feminist theologians challenge this legacy, offering new interpretations that affirm the dignity and worth of all people. They uncover how scripture has been used to silence women and subordinate them. But new biblical interpretations and methods from postcolonial, queer, Black, and other theologies are being used to enrich feminist biblical interpretations and make them more inclusive, complex, and nuanced. As the book challenges patriarchal readings which oppress women, the book also offers liberative ways of approaching, reading, interpreting, and living out the scriptures.

This book introduces readers to a variety (though not all) of feminist theologies: Asian American, Womanist Queer, Postcolonial, Eco-feminist, African, Latina, and Disability. Each feminist theology is a powerful response to the overlapping systems of oppression that women continue to face. These theologies help us see that women's suffering is not monolithic and cannot be addressed with a one-size-fits-all theology. Instead, each theology speaks to specific contexts, offering deep insights into the layers of injustice that must be dismantled.

At their core, feminist theologies call us back to the Gospel message, a message of liberation, equity, justice, and hope. They invite us to reimagine our faith in ways that are not just reflective, but transformative. Through feminist theology, we gain a deeper understanding of God, of spirituality, each other, the planet, and ourselves. We learn that all people are beloved children of God. We are invited to live into that truth by reshaping our communities, our churches, and our world. This work is not complete, but it is ongoing. And we are all invited to continue the work so that the future generations of women will experience equality and justice. The insights and practices offered in this book are not just for theological reflection but are meant to shape our daily lives, our activism, and our communities.

We are all invited to join in this important ongoing work of gender equality and justice. Through these various feminist theologies, we can help build a world where liberation is not a dream but a reality for women, for all people, and for the Earth itself. Let us continue the journey toward justice, toward liberation, and toward a world where every woman, every person, and all of creation can truly flourish.

INDEX

19th Amendment 25

AAPI 37, 57
able-bodied 8, 16, 32, 173, 175, 176, 179, 181
ableism 89, 173, 175–179, 181, 182, 185, 188, 189
Aboriginal 43
Africa 39, 106, 137, 140, 142, 143; colonization 138–139; HIV/AIDS in Africa 145–146; same-sex relationships in Africa 148–149
African 24, 34, 84; African biblical interpretation 38–39; African women's theologies 137–154
Althaus-Reid, Marcella 134, 135, 161–162, 171, 172
Anti-blackness 34, 81
Anzaldúa, Gloria 124
Aquino, Maria Pilar 128, 135
Asanti, Ta'Shia 77
Asian American(s) 36–37, 51, 53, 55–59, 62, 69, 70, 74; biblical interpretation 36–38; feminist theologies 51–72

Baker-Fletcher, Karen 76, 85
beauty standards 62–63
Belser, Julia Watts 178, 183, 186
Betcher, Sharon V. 174, 180, 186

Bible 3, 8. 9. 15, 16, 17, 21, 64, 68, 77, 83, 87, 90, 95, 117, 140, 148, 149, 151, 168, 169, 189; African feminist interpretation of the Bible 141–143; feminist perspectives on the Bible 23–50; Latina feminist interpretation of the Bible 132–133; postcolonial readings of the Bible 109–112; queering the Bible 162–167
biblical criticism 3, 16, 28, 44, 110, 141
biblical inerrantists 25
biblical interpretation 11, 24, 27, 64, 85, 112, 139; African feminist biblical interpretation 38–39, 141–143; Asian and Asian American feminist interpretation 36–38; Dalit feminist biblical interpretation 39–40; eco-feminist biblical interpretation 46–48; Indigenous feminist biblical interpretation 42–43; intersectional feminist biblical interpretation 33–34; Jewish feminist biblical interpretation 41–42; Latina feminist biblical interpretation 132–133; Mujerista and Latina feminist biblical interpretation 35–36;

Palestinian feminist biblical interpretation 40–41; postcolonial feminist biblical interpretation 44–45; queer biblical interpretation 45–46; womanist biblical interpretation 34–35
biblical literalism 3, 25–26
bisexual 155
Black Church 73, 74, 75, 78. 80, 83–85
bodies 62, 68, 78, 81, 91, 98, 130, 145, 147, 148, 149, 155, 156, 157, 158, 160, 161, 169, 170, 171; Black Bodies 81, 159; disabled Bodies 170, 173, 174, 177, 179, 182, 183; queer Bodies 158, 159; trans bodies 169, 174, 180; women's bodies 62, 78, 79, 91, 148, 173, 177, 180
body of Christ 18, 66, 83, 160, 161, 170, 185
body of God 97, 99, 150
Bong, Sharon 159, 171
Bosadi 140, 153
Botho/ubuntu 38, 140
Brock, Rita Nakashima 63
Buddhist 40, 137
Bultmann, Rudolph 27

Cable Act 52
Canaanite woman 43
Cannon, Katie 74, 85
Carroll, Sefora 92, 93, 94, 104
Catholic Church 2, 125, 149
Cheng, Patrick 70, 71, 167
Chi 65, 68
Chinese 52, 58
Christ 13, 38, 40, 66, 79–80, 83, 98, 118, 119, 146, 158, 160, 163, 183, 185
Christian nationalism 89
Christology 76, 146, 147
cis-gender 8, 11, 12, 16, 44, 120, 159, 170

Claassens, Juliana 28, 48
Clare-Young, Alex 169, 171
classism 38, 77, 80, 89, 119, 123, 140, 181, 182
Cleveland, Christena 78, 79, 81, 86
climate change 46–48, 87, 91–95, 96, 99, 101, 102, 103, 104, 149, 151
colonialism 14, 26, 38, 39, 41, 44, 63, 66, 89, 92, 93, 96, 100, 106, 107–108, 109, 110, 112, 114, 116, 117, 119, 120, 121, 123, 138, 144, 145, 148, 149
colonizers 24, 43, 45, 106, 107, 108, 109, 142
coming Out 45, 46, 158, 166
Cone, James 78
Conquest 3, 42, 44, 45, 106, 108, 111, 117, 123
contextual theology 107, 123, 188
Copeland, Shawn 80, 86
Cornwall, Susannah 159, 170–171, 172
COVID-19 pandemic 37, 57
creation 32, 47, 48, 66, 69, 87–89, 90, 92, 93, 97, 98, 99, 100, 101, 102, 104, 115, 116, 148, 150, 151, 163, 164, 167, 186, 190
Cross 18, 35, 85, 143; womanist understandings 82–83
cultural whiteness 55

Daly, Mary 13
Dalit 39, 40, 49
dangerous memory 30, 31
decolonize 108, 111, 116, 117, 158
desire xi, 12, 23, 33, 51, 53, 57, 63, 76, 83, 88, 95, 102, 109, 111, 114, 121, 122, 131, 132, 134, 150
diasporic imagination 120

dignity 63, 74, 133, 144, 147, 163, 178, 189
Dinah 29
disability/ies 9, 173–189; medical model of disability; social model of disability 175
disabled bodies 170, 173, 174, 177, 179, 182, 183
disabled Christ 183, 185
disabled God 183, 187
Doctrine of Discovery 24
domination 16, 19, 21, 44, 56, 82, 89, 91, 96, 107, 116, 123, 155, 163
Donaldson, Laura 42, 49
Douglas, Kelly Brown 76, 79, 80, 81, 82, 84, 86
drag 95
dualism 97, 166, 174
Dube, Musa W. 39, 45, 49, 109, 111, 113, 116–119, 121, 138, 140–142, 148, 152, 153

Earth 17, 23, 47, 48, 85, 87–93, 96–103, 105, 149–151, 180
ecclesiology 18, 130
ecology 90, 103, 104, 153
Edet, Rosemary 139, 153
Eiesland, Nancy 183
Ekeya, Bette 139, 153
empire 1, 8, 10, 24, 44, 45, 47, 83, 101, 106, 108, 109, 111, 116, 119, 121, 122, 134, 163
empowerment 23, 37, 61, 69, 71, 118, 135, 141, 143, 175, 189
enslavement 14, 24, 52, 77–79, 108
environment 1, 23, 37, 88–92, 94–98, 100, 103, 149, 153, 188
equality 9, 16, 18, 40, 44, 56, 93, 107, 120, 129, 131, 142, 190
eschatology 40, 47, 48, 50, 99–103, 105, 128
Espinoza, Robert Che 134, 135

ethics: feminist ethics of care 184, 185; feminist disability ethics 184–186
Eucharist 40, 160
Eurocentric 68, 116
exploitation 34, 54, 66, 84, 90, 100, 106, 123, 137, 138, 139, 144, 145
Ezer kenegdo 32

feminist disability theorists 177
feminist theory 109, 177, 179
Fuchs, Esther 42

Gafney, Wil 35, 78, 85, 86
gay 12, 70, 71, 94, 145, 154–156, 159
Gebara, Ivone 88, 91, 92, 104
gender xi, 3–19, 27–29, 32, 34, 38–42, 44–45, 49, 52, 53, 56, 57, 60, 61, 63, 73, 74, 77, 85, 91–95, 107, 109, 112, 116, 119–123, 133, 135, 138–141, 143, 144, 147, 148, 154–161, 168–172, 174, 177, 179, 182, 185, 189, 190
gender binary 4, 155, 156, 171
globalization 90, 102, 106
González, Justo L. 125, 135
Gonzalez, Michelle 124
Grant, Jacquelyn 31, 80, 86

Hagar 28, 30
Hall-Smith, Beverly Moana 43, 49
Hammer, Jill 42, 49
Han 38
Harris, Melanie L. 89, 104
hermeneutics of remembrance 30
hermeneutics of suspicion 30
heteronormativity 45, 46, 121, 156, 161, 171,
heteropatriarchy 19, 34, 94, 186
heterosexism 45, 48, 77, 79, 80, 89, 114, 123, 181, 182, 189

heterosexual 4, 5, 8, 11, 16, 32, 45, 46, 145, 148, 155–157, 159, 161, 165, 170, 171
heterosexuality 4, 45, 155, 157, 159, 161, 170, 171
hierarchy 4, 12, 53, 56, 58, 81, 160, 161, 164
Hill Collins, Patricia 20
Hipsher, B. K. 169, 172
HIV/AIDS 84, 145, 146, 148, 154, 164, 180
Hokmah 17
homophobia 18, 45, 48, 70, 77, 84, 106, 148
hooks, bell 34
hybrid theology 117, 118
hybridity 18, 110, 112–118, 122
hypersexualized 57
hypervisibility 61

Immigration Act 53
imperialism 20, 21, 24, 39, 44, 46, 48, 90, 96, 108, 109, 111, 117, 119, 120, 141–143
indecent theology 134, 135, 161, 171
infanticide 178
intersections 6, 7, 10, 14, 19, 20, 45, 60, 77, 79, 81, 95, 117, 123, 133, 140, 156, 161, 179, 181, 185, 188
intersectionality 1, 5, 19, 21, 22, 70, 122
intersex 6, 170, 171
invisibility 25, 37, 61, 62, 65, 66, 67, 69, 106, 179
Isasi-Diaz, Ada Maria 35, 36, 49, 127, 131, 132, 135
Isherwood, Lisa 146, 153, 172, 184, 187

Jeong 65, 67, 68
Johnson, Elizabeth 17, 22, 88, 105
Julian of Norwich 2, 15

Kanongata, Keiti Ann 99
Kanyoro, Musimbi 142, 153
Kenosis 150
kenotic 150, 151, 153
kenotic theology 150, 151
Kim, Grace Ji-Sun 50, 55, 65, 66, 67, 68, 69, 71, 105, 113, 122, 153
Kittay, Eva Feder 186, 187
Kwok, Pui-lan 49, 50, 58, 63, 64, 71, 108, 118, 120, 121, 122, 154
Kyung, Chung Hyun 64

La Raza 133
La vida cotidiana 127
Latina feminist 123, 124, 126–129, 131–133, 135
Lee, Jung Young 71
lesbian 4, 77, 133, 155, 156, 159
LGBTQI+ 4, 8, 14, 23, 24, 45, 70, 77, 94–96, 106, 112, 118, 134, 155, 159, 162, 167, 180
liberation theology 124, 129, 134
Lorde, Audre 34, 75

machismo 123
marginality 124
Mary, the sister of Martha 31
May, Vivian 20
McFague, Sallie 17, 96, 98, 103, 105, 149
Mestiza 113, 126, 135
midrash 42
Minjung 37, 38, 49
misogyny 21, 85, 106, 147, 156
model minority 57, 58
Mollenkott, Virginia Ramey 169, 172
moral 27, 35, 75, 79, 82, 127, 129, 175, 180
Morrison, Toni 34
Mother Earth 149–151
Mujerista 35, 36, 49, 123, 126, 127, 131, 133, 135

Mujerista theologies 123, 126
multiculturalism 113, 124

naturalized 53
non-binary 12, 171
normalcy 177, 179
Nortjé-Meyer, Lily 90, 105

Oceania 92, 93, 99, 104
Oduyoye, Mercy 137, 143, 146, 148, 152–154
ordinary readers 39, 44, 141
Orpah 46, 49, 166
Othering 63, 179, 180
Ou-ri 65, 68

Park, A. Sung 49
patriarchy 7, 9, 12, 16, 18, 21, 23, 26, 28–30, 32–34, 38, 42, 46, 53–54, 67, 78, 85, 91, 94, 95, 11, 116, 119, 137, 139, 142–145, 151, 157, 173–174, 181, 182, 186, 189
people of color 4, 8, 14, 57–59, 79, 159, 178, 180
Perichoresis 143
Plaskow, Judith 41, 42, 49, 50
Pneuma 68
postcolonialism 107, 112, 119, 121, 122
postmodernism 4, 5
praxis 19, 35, 110, 113, 123, 142, 150
preferential option for the poor 129
Prentis, Brooke 43, 50
process theology 183

queer feminist theology 155, 156, 158, 172
queer sexualities 148, 166
queer theory 105, 134, 135, 155, 159, 160
queerness 94, 95, 148, 159, 160, 171

race/ethnicity 120, 123, 133, 156, 158
racialization 55
racism 34, 36–38, 48, 51, 52–58, 61–63, 65–67, 69, 70, 73, 74, 77, 79–81, 84, 89, 100, 114, 119, 123, 125, 140, 181, 186, 188
resistance 10, 18, 19, 29–31, 42, 43, 45, 61, 74, 113–115, 118, 128, 129, 157, 158
resurrection 27, 46, 82, 83, 169, 181, 183, 185
Reuther, Rosemary Radford 18, 22
Roman Empire 1, 101, 111, 163
Rossing, Barbara 47, 48, 50, 100, 101, 105
Ruach 68
Russell, Letty 18, 22

Sacred Black Feminine 78, 85
same-sex relationships 148, 165, 166
Schüssler Fiorenza, Elisabeth 30, 50
Second Wave 9, 16–18
sexual assault 79, 91, 92, 176
sexuality xi, 1, 5–8, 10, 19, 20, 34, 45, 60, 70, 71, 76, 94, 109, 120, 121, 123, 133, 143, 144, 145, 148, 149, 154, 155–158, 160–164, 167, 169, 171, 174, 182, 184, 188
Shiphrah and Puah 36
silence 23, 30, 56, 61, 82, 139, 189
sin 1, 9, 10, 18, 35, 48, 66, 67, 70, 71, 80, 81, 84, 86, 89, 100, 127, 128, 144–146, 165, 180, 183
Sodom 164, 165
Sophia 17, 71
Southern Baptist 13, 22

spirit 12, 17, 43, 65, 68, 71, 84, 93, 97, 130, 131, 138, 151, 157, 160, 167, 169, 173, 174
spirituality 63, 64, 76, 86, 93, 138, 144, 154, 156, 189
Stanton, Elizabeth Cady 9
stereotypes 14, 16, 34, 169, 176, 177, 179, 181
storytelling 38–40, 49, 120, 139, 141
structural sin 35, 48, 100, 127, 128
submission 3, 12, 14, 26, 139, 144, 161
syncretism 64, 115, 117, 129
systematic theology 1–4, 8

Tamez, Elsa 136
teología de jotería 134
texts of terror 28
Torah 41, 42
Townes, Emilie 75, 86
trans theologies 167, 169, 170
transgender 12, 158, 168, 169, 172
Treaty of Waitangi 43, 49
Trible, Phyllis 28
Truth, Sojourner 9, 22
Turman, Eboni Marshall 73, 86

Ubuntu 38, 84, 85, 140, 144
utopian 102, 131, 132

violence, sexual 176

Walker, Alice 34, 74, 86
War Brides Act 53
West, Mona 50, 166, 172
White supremacy 26, 79, 189
Williams, Delores 34, 75, 76, 81, 82, 84, 86
womanism 34, 73, 74, 83, 85
Woman's Bible 9
Womb of God 151
women of color 19, 60, 89, 116, 117
Women's Movement 9

Zaru, Jean 41, 50

For Product Safety Concerns and Information please contact our EU representative GPSR@taylorandfrancis.com
Taylor & Francis Verlag GmbH, Kaufingerstraße 24, 80331 München, Germany

www.ingramcontent.com/pod-product-compliance
Lightning Source LLC
Chambersburg PA
CBHW071741150426
43191CB00010B/1651